ASEA Cell Performance:

REDOXEnergy • REDOXMind • REDOXMood

Feel good about feeling good

ASEA's Cell Performance products have been developed based on redox principles, so we don't have to rely on artificial additives. Instead, we leverage proprietary ingredient blends that help your body's performance.

No artificial flavors   **No artificial colors**   **No artificial sugars**   **No artificial preservatives**

Take a packet with you wherever you go and drink when convenient.

Our powdered mix is easy to travel with and simple to use.

Just open and add one stick pack to your preferred beverage.

Shake or stir to incorporate and drink all the contents. Adjust the type of beverage or amount of liquid for more or less flavor.

Ever feel tired?

Fight fatigue with sustained cellular energy.

Try **REDOXEnergy**

Ingredients that support cellular performance. REDOXEnergy's blend of Powered by Redox™ ingredients ignites sustained physical and mental energy by helping your cells reach redox balance.*

Proprietary REDOXEnergy blend

Natural Guarana - Guarana provides the energy you need to be alert while supporting cellular redox balance. See improved alertness with this natural source of caffeine.* Less caffeine than a cup of coffee.

L-Theanine - L-theanine has been shown to improve your focus and boost your mood, while promoting brain cell and neuro protection.*

Vitamin B3- Supports your body's natural energy levels and protects your cells.*

Supporting Energy blend

Ginseng extract - Combats oxidative stress which boosts cognitive energy output.*

Vitamin B6, B12 - Supports your body's natural energy levels and protects your cells.*

36|86

Ever feel brain fog? Give your brain a boost – think clearly and focus more easily.

Try **REDOX**Mind

REDOXMind helps improve cognitive health through Powered by Redox™ ingredients that support your brain's performance at the cellular level, keeping your mind sharp.*

Proprietary REDOXMind blend

Red Orange Complex - Helps positively regulate glutathione (GSH) levels and antioxidant enzymes to support the ability for learning and improved memory—specifically spatial and recognition memory.*

Nicotinamide mononucleotide - Supports against brain cell disruptions and helps your brain age in a healthy way.*

Supporting Mind blend

Zinc - Helps manage brain chemicals, shortening response time and alleviating mental stress so you can stay focused and sharp.*

Nootropic Blend - Supports neurotransmitter functions to help your brain retrieve and relay information.*

Ever feel anxiety or overwhelmed?

Improve your mood and let everyday stress slip away.

Try **REDOX**Mood

Ingredients that support cellular performance

Feel calm and balanced anytime with REDOXMood's proprietary blend of Powered by Redox™ ingredients.*

Proprietary REDOXMood blend

GABA - Enhances neurotransmitter levels that help regulate mood, reduces oxidative stress in the central nervous system, and improves redox balance.

L-Tyrosine - Supports elevated expression of redox enzymes to help regulate mood.

Supporting Mood blend

Rhodiola Rosea and Ashwagandha - Helps your body regulate stress hormones to create a feeling of relaxation.

Saffron - Supports fighting stress for better sleep, leading to improved overall mood.

B Vitamins and natural herbs - Helps regulate your stress hormones to improve relaxation.

WHY WE NEED
THE GIFTS OF THE

RICK RENNER

Harrison
House

Tulsa, OK.

Why We Need the Gifts of the Holy Spirit
ISBN: 978-1-68031-223-2
Copyright © 2018 by Rick Renner
8316 E. 73rd St.
Tulsa, OK 74133

Published by Harrison House Publishers
Tulsa, OK 74145
www.harrisonhouse.com

3 4 5 / 23 22 21

Editorial Consultants: Cynthia D. Hansen, Rebecca L. Gilbert
Text Design: Lisa Simpson,
  www.SimpsonProductions.net
Cover: Debbie Pullman, Zoe Life Creative Media
  Design@ZoeLifeCreative.com, www.ZoeLifeCreative.com

CONTENTS

PREFACE

My purpose in writing this book is to take a fresh look at the gifts of the Holy Spirit — to explore why we need them and what they produce in the life of a church and in the life of each believer. I'm a very logical kind of thinker, so I have written this book from that point of view. I endeavor to answer these two questions: Logically, why did God give His Church the gifts of the Holy Spirit? And given the answer to that question, why then do we need to make space for them to operate among us?

The New Testament makes it abundantly clear that the Holy Spirit is loaded with spiritual gifts that He wants to manifest in the life of a local church. These gifts are from the Holy Spirit, intentionally given to the Body of Christ for specific purposes, so they are vital and needed in *every* congregation. Some churches, however, have gone so long without making room for the manifestation of these gifts that they don't even know *how* to make room for them anymore.

I have observed that the majority of large churches today allow very little time for the manifestation of the gifts of the Holy Spirit. The reason is partially due to the multiple services that so many churches hold, which creates a time constraint in getting people in and out before the next service begins. I completely understand that dilemma, and I know how important it is to make space for as many people as possible.

But in the process of making space for people, we cannot forget to make space for the Holy Spirit as well.

Perhaps you are exploring — or revisiting — your need to more fully accommodate the moving of the Spirit in your life. I pray that this book is a blessing to you. It's not a deep, scholarly

> **In the process of making space for people, we cannot forget to make space for the Holy Spirit as well.**

work, but it is intended to walk you through the primary reasons we *must* have the gifts of the Holy Spirit demonstrated in our midst. I believe the insights you glean from this teaching will help you see that the operation of these spiritual gifts really is not optional if we want to grow in the grace and power of the Lord Jesus Christ.

Rick Renner

INTRODUCTION

Are you hungry to know and experience more of the supernatural working of the Holy Spirit in your life? If you are, you'll be happy to know that God desires that for you more than you do yourself. He has dimensions of His power and gifts that He has designed to operate both in your life personally and in your local church.

Before we discuss the gifts of the Holy Spirit, I want to begin by saying that these spiritual gifts are normally activated in the life of a believer *after* he or she receives the baptism in the Holy Spirit. This experience, which is subsequent to salvation, opens the door for a person to operate in the power of God and in the supernatural workings of the Holy Spirit's gifts. When a person repents of sin and receives Christ as Lord, the Holy Spirit instantly indwells that person's born-again spirit and produces peace in his or her heart. But when a person subsequently receives the baptism in the Holy Spirit, His infilling presence unleashes a flood of divine power to empower and enable a believer to operate mightily in spiritual gifts for the benefit of man and the furtherance of God's Kingdom.

If you have never received this glorious subsequent experience called the baptism in the Holy Spirit, I encourage you to ask the Lord to receive that gift today (*see* page 86, "Prayer To Receive the Baptism in the Holy Spirit"). As you receive this powerful encounter with God's Spirit, you will also receive a new ability to pray in tongues — a heavenly language given by the Holy Spirit as He prays through you.

This is why the baptism in the Holy Spirit has been called the "door to the supernatural." On the other side of that door, there is so much more awaiting you as you learn to walk closely with the Holy Spirit and yield to His promptings. He desires to release divine, supernatural gifts in your life — which is the subject of this book.

So let's turn our attention to the nine gifts of the Holy Spirit that are found in First Corinthians 12. Our goal is to better understand why we need these spiritual gifts, what they produce in the midst of God's people, and whether He intends for these divine enablements to operate in the lives of believers today. I believe that what you are about to read will provide you with a fresh approach to this wonderful, powerful subject.

A whole realm of the supernatural awaits you!

I thank my God always on your behalf,
for the grace of God
which is given you by Jesus Christ;
That in every thing ye are enriched by him,
in all utterance, and in all knowledge;
Even as the testimony of Christ
was confirmed in you:
So that ye come behind in no gift;
waiting for the coming
of our Lord Jesus Christ:
Who shall also confirm you unto the end,
that ye may be blameless
in the day of our Lord Jesus Christ.
God is faithful, by whom ye were called
unto the fellowship
of his Son Jesus Christ our Lord.
— 1 Corinthians 1:4-9

CHAPTER ONE

A FRESH LOOK AT THE GIFTS OF THE HOLY SPIRIT

*W*hen I was growing up, I attended a wonderful church, but we did not believe in present-day gifts of the Holy Spirit. Actually, at that time, the official position of our denomination was that the gifts of the Holy Spirit had unquestionably been a part of the Early Church in its formative years but had passed away with the death of the apostles. Perhaps you were reared in a similar traditional church and were taught as I was.

I'm thankful for the church where I grew up. My pastor loved the Bible and taught it well. He and the church family taught me to be committed to Christ and instructed me in my responsibility to witness to others. We all worked and prayed together to build a strong church family. My own family served in Sunday school and in Training Union (a Sunday night class for youth), and we sang from our hearts in the various church choirs. In so many ways, my memories of my local church are wonderful. Those early years in that church helped formed the foundation for my present-day ministry, the bedrock of most of my doctrinal beliefs, and the basis for much of what I believe about the importance of the local church today.

But as lovely as so many of my experiences were in my local church, one crucial element was missing: *the supernatural working of the gifts of the Holy Spirit.* Today I know this work of the Holy Spirit well, but it was absent in the church where I grew up because we didn't believe in the present-day experience of the baptism of the Holy Spirit, nor in the present-day operation of the gifts of the Holy Spirit.

Because our church didn't believe in the manifestations of these spiritual gifts in this present day, we basically deemed Pentecostals and Charismatics to be doctrinally off-based. We believed that whatever it was that they were claiming to experience, those experiences were merely foolish, made-up works of the flesh based on bad doctrine and a mishandling of Scripture.

DOES THE HOLY SPIRIT MAKE A CHURCH CARNAL?

I vividly remember a series of messages preached in our church in which we were told that the carnality in the church at Corinth was a perfect illustration of modern-day Pentecostal and Charismatic excesses. The point was argued that the church at Corinth was more carnal than any of the other churches of New Testament *because* of their emphasis on the baptism in the Holy Spirit and the gifts of the Holy Spirit. That message was pounded into our minds again and again — that these gifts eventually caused the church in Corinth to become silly and childish.

There is no question that the Corinthian congregation had problems with carnal behavior, and shortly I'll cover the reason for these issues of carnality. Paul clearly referred to these problems in his first and second epistles to the church in Corinth. But as I listened to this argument that the gifts of the Holy Spirit *caused* the Corinthian believers' silliness and carnality, I wondered, *Was their carnality a result of the working of the Holy Spirit? Would God actually give spiritual gifts to cause people to be immature and carnal?*

Even as a young teenager, I came to a clear conclusion regarding these inward questions: *Of course not!* The Holy Spirit is *never* the source of immaturity and carnality.

As I continued over the course of many years to study the epistles to the Corinthian church, I reached my own conclusions about what contributed to the behavior of some its members. I came to understand that the carnality within the Corinthian congregation was *not* caused by the gifts of the Holy Spirit that worked among them; in reality, that carnality was probably *exposed* because of those spiritual gifts.

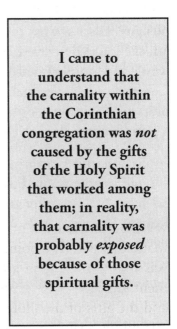

I came to understand that the carnality within the Corinthian congregation was *not* caused by the gifts of the Holy Spirit that worked among them; in reality, that carnality was probably *exposed* because of those spiritual gifts.

A survey of the New Testament and early Christian history shows that all the churches of the First Century had problems with carnality. At that time, most Christians were getting saved out of a pagan world filled with immorality, drunkenness, and carnality of every type. These early converts carried much of that old baggage into their new life in Christ. That is the reason Paul had to instruct the churches in all his letters on how to deal with and overcome various issues of carnality. Even the more mature church of Ephesus seemed to have a problem with drunkenness (*see* Ephesians 5:18).

Often the Corinthian church is portrayed as being the most carnal of all New Testament churches. In his letters, the apostle Paul certainly addressed the issue of carnality in the church (*see* 1 Corinthians 3:1-4; 2 Corinthians 12:21). But was it *really* the case that it was the *most* carnal?

History of the Church at Corinth

Let me give you a little history of the church at Corinth so you can gain a better understanding of why this congregation has often been labeled as the most carnal church of early New Testament times. Historical information provides needed insight to help explain why this particular church had so many issues.

The city of Corinth was a very old city that had previously rebelled against the authority of Rome. As a result, Rome attacked and destroyed the city in 146 BC, and its ruins lay in waste and uninhabited for many years. Then in 44 BC, Julius Caesar decided to reestablish Corinth as a Roman colony because of its advantageous position on the narrow isthmus that served as a "land bridge" linking central and southern Greece.

Rebuilding Corinth proved to be a challenge because not enough people wanted to relocate to these old, devastated ruins. So Julius Caesar offered the incentive of a new life to veteran Roman legionnaires (soldiers), as well as to the poor and freed slaves of Rome. Caesar promised free land if these people would relocate to Corinth, help reconstruct it, and become the new city leaders. As a result of this offer, large numbers of these groups of people moved to Corinth and became the founding fathers of the newly emerging city.

The Greek goddess Aphrodite was prominent in the older version of Corinth, and Julius Caesar believed he was a direct descendent of the goddess. So it was a natural choice for Caesar to dedicate the new city of Corinth to Aphrodite. And since Aphrodite was revered as the goddess of sex and of prostitutes, the sex industry again came to play a major role in the reconstructed city, just as it had in the Corinth of centuries earlier. Among many pagan temples, a significant temple was built to the worship of Aphrodite, and the sex industry flourished in a city that was filled with a large population of lower-class freedmen and tough, seasoned legionnaires.

The city was also located between two ports, one on the west coast to receive ships from Rome, and another on the east coast to receive ships from Asia and beyond. Because of the city's sex industry, it became a tourist stop for sailors and travelers who arrived at these ports and then made their way into Corinth to indulge in sexual pleasures.

In addition, Corinth was also widely known for its culture of drunken debauchery. The excessive use of alcohol by Corinthians was so notorious that if a person lived in the Roman world and was a drunkard, it is likely that person would have been referred to as a "Corinthian." In fact, the term "to Corinthianize" came to refer to engaging in debaucheries of all types — sexual sin as well as drunkenness. The portrayal of actors as drunk Corinthians was widely practiced throughout the Roman Empire. Such was the reputation of Corinthians across the Roman world in the First Century. They were generally thought of as lower-class, crude, fornicating drunkards.

Furthermore, not far from Corinth were the Panhellenic Games of ancient Greece. Because Corinth was the city closest to the site of these games, it became the official host of the games and thereby benefited from revenue generated from people who came from all over the Roman world to participate in or view the games. Of course, the large numbers of visitors to the games contributed to the growth of the sex industry, the sale of alcohol, and to the tourist business in general. These Panhellenic Games were highly competitive games, and as a result, a prevailing spirit of competition also affected the mindset of Corinthians and helped build the city's reputation as one marked by fierce competition.

Because the city was filled with people seeking a new future, it also attracted fortune hunters who wanted to make a quick and easy buck. Professional swindlers saw this as a great opportunity, so they, too, arrived in large numbers.

If you mix all of these components together, it paints quite a picture of First Century Corinth. It was a city of strategic location that offered unrestricted sex, limitless consumption of alcohol, and a fierce spirit of competition. It was a city largely populated by coarse, immoral soldiers, sailors, and freedmen, with a large dose of charlatans, swindlers, and cheaters added to the mix. When all of these ingredients are resident in one place and all restraint is thrown to the wind — the result is a city like the ancient city of Corinth.

That was the makeup of Corinth when Christ came into the world, when the Church newly emerged after His resurrection, and when Paul later started a church there. It stands to reason that the citizenry would be the audience Paul was reaching with the Gospel as he preached within the city limits. And those who responded to the truth of that message were the people with whom he started his new congregation.

This is the reason for Paul's description of who the Corinthian believers were before they came to Christ: "Know ye not that the unrighteous shall not inherit the kingdom of God? Be not deceived: neither fornicators, nor idolaters, nor adulterers, nor effeminate, nor abusers of themselves with mankind, nor thieves, nor covetous, nor drunkards, nor revilers, nor extortioners, shall inherit the kingdom of God. And such were some of you..." (1 Corinthians 6:9-11).

Paul's words describe precisely who the people in the church at Corinth were before they came to Christ. It was a congregation full of individuals with a morally lurid past.

This explains the prevalence of carnality that existed in the Corinthian church. If you read the issues that the apostle Paul addressed in his two epistles to the congregation, you will discover that the believers were still dealing with sexual sin, alcohol abuse, competition among themselves, and people taking advantage of one another.

This also helps us understand why Paul wrote the Corinthian church in such a strong and direct manner compared to the way he addressed other congregations. These were people raised in a culture known for its coarseness, so Paul's communication with them had to be conducted in a manner they would understand and respond to. Speaking gently would not have been effective in addressing this particular group, so Paul wrote in a firmer, more forthright manner to the Corinthian believers.

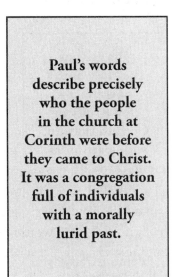

Paul's words describe precisely who the people in the church at Corinth were before they came to Christ. It was a congregation full of individuals with a morally lurid past.

For all these reasons, the Corinthian congregation seemed to have more prominent problems than other churches; however, it was simply a result of how these believers had lived before they came to Christ. They were still in the process of overcoming their carnal practices and learning to live transformed lives.

SOME GIFTS OF THE HOLY SPIRIT BRING ISSUES TO THE SURFACE

Through the years, I continued to ponder more deeply the situation in the church of Corinth compared to other New Testament churches. Eventually I came to understand that Corinth, even with all of its problems, was not that much worse off than other New Testament churches. Those problems were simply more *exposed* at Corinth.

In spite of all the carnal issues that lingered in the church in Corinth, this didn't hinder the gifts of the Holy Spirit from operating mightily among them. In fact, the gifts of the Holy Spirit operated so powerfully in Corinth that sin, wrong attitudes, and carnality were supernaturally brought to the surface. Through these demonstrations of the Spirit, whatever needed to be addressed was exposed and dealt with *God's* way. The sin that might stay hidden below the surface in other churches could not remain hidden in Corinth, because the abundant flow of the revelatory gifts of the Spirit at that church ensured that it *would* become exposed.

> The gifts of the Holy Spirit operated so powerfully in Corinth that sin, wrong attitudes, and carnality were supernaturally brought to the surface. Through these demonstrations of the Spirit, whatever needed to be addressed was exposed and dealt with *God's* way.

This is a significant point to understand, because it means the gifts of the Spirit were *not* the source of the Corinthian believers' problems, as some allege. Rather, it was actually the gifts of the Holy Spirit that *brought these sinful issues to light* so God could *purge* the sin from their midst. The strong operation of the gifts of the Spirit served as God's instrument to bring conviction and correction; then those same gifts contributed to guiding the believers to a new level of spiritual maturity.

For example, in First Corinthians 14:24 and 25, Paul taught that the gift of prophecy brings sinful attitudes to light so they can be exposed and corrected by the Spirit of God. The truth is, where an abundance of gifts of the Holy Spirit is at work, it is more likely that wrong attitudes, sin, and carnal behavior will be exposed. Not all the gifts of the Spirit are revelatory in nature. However, they do all come from the Spirit of Truth, and they serve the purpose of edifying the discouraged and downtrodden, righting things that are wrong, and bringing hidden things to light. As you will see in the chapters that follow, Paul actually taught that we *must* have the nine gifts of the Holy Spirit in order to bring the Church into spiritual maturity.

It is a fact that where the Holy Spirit is moving powerfully, He often addresses issues of sin and wrong attitudes. First, the Holy Spirit speaks privately to an individual's heart. But if a sinful situation has become so full-blown that it is affecting an entire congregation, it is not unusual for the Holy Spirit to address it publicly, either through an inspired message preached by the pastor, or through a revelatory gift of the Spirit, which we will discuss later in this book. In such cases, the Holy Spirit's objective is to address the issue and thereby bring the congregation to a position of repentance and cleansing.

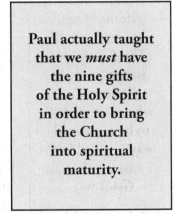

Paul actually taught that we *must* have the nine gifts of the Holy Spirit in order to bring the Church into spiritual maturity.

So the insinuation that the gifts of the Spirit produce carnality simply cannot pass scriptural muster. Nor does the claim that the gifts of the Spirit passed away with the death of the apostles hold any merit. We'll see in the following chapter that Paul explicitly taught that these spiritual gifts are *essential* for the Church and that God's plan is for such spiritual manifestations to richly endow the Church *until* the coming of the Lord Jesus Christ.

As you will see, the gifts of the Holy Spirit are *vital* for the fullness of Christ to operate in the Church. When they are absent, a crucial supernatural element is missing in the midst of God's people.

Unfortunately, even many Pentecostal and Charismatic churches have backed away from the gifts of the Holy Spirit in recent times. The unspoken implication is that it's not cool to be known as people who speak in tongues or to associate with people who operate in the gifts of the Holy Spirit. This is a true tragedy, for when these spiritual gifts are missing from the church, the outcome is a church functioning primarily on the strength of human effort, reasoning, and talent.

> Hidden sin tends to remain hidden in a church that lacks the operation of spiritual gifts, becoming a silent poison to the spiritual atmosphere of the church. This type of situation eventually causes apathy, undermines the church's prayer life, and stymies growth, eating away at the life of that local body and its ability to fulfill its particular assignment within God's larger plan.

When the gifts of the Holy Spirit are absent, the Church experiences less spiritual vitality and effectiveness. In addition, hidden sin — such as the problems revealed in the Corinthian congregation — tends to remain hidden in a church that lacks the operation of spiritual gifts, becoming a silent poison to the spiritual atmosphere of the church. This type of situation eventually causes apathy, undermines the church's prayer life, and stymies growth, eating away at the life of that local body and its ability to fulfill its particular assignment within God's larger plan.

That's why it's so important that we take a fresh look at the nine gifts of the Spirit. We must embrace these supernatural manifestations, knowing that God gave them to the Body of Christ because we *need* them. He never intended for the gifts of the

Holy Spirit to be a cause for embarrassment. He gave them to make us smarter and sharper! God wants the gifts of His Spirit to impart supernatural wisdom and revelation to us. He designed them to take us higher and to enable us to demonstrate His love and His power on the earth!

In the following chapters, we're going to study the nature of the nine gifts of the Spirit found in First Corinthians 12 and why they are so important to the Church. But before we do, we should also note that two other categories of spiritual gifts are found in Paul's epistles. Romans 12:6-8 lists what many call the *motivational gifts*: prophecy, serving, teaching, exhortation, giving, administration, and mercy. Each of us is given at least one of these motivational gifts by the Holy Spirit as foundational inner motivations that help us fulfill His purpose in our lives.

The other category of spiritual gifts is the fivefold ministry gifts found in Ephesians 4:11: apostle, prophet, evangelist, pastor, and teacher. These ministry offices are given to the Body "for the perfecting of the saints, for the work of the ministry, for the edifying of the body of Christ" (Ephesians 4:12). But let's focus now on the nine gifts of the Spirit listed in First Corinthians 12:8-10 to see what they are and how they operate in the Church.

The Bible teaches very clearly that the nine gifts of the Holy Spirit are *essential* in order for us to be the supernatural Church that God intends. So let's proceed to see what the New Testament teaches about these nine spiritual gifts and the reasons we *must* have them actively operating in our midst right up to the return of our Lord Jesus Christ!

> **The nine gifts of the Holy Spirit are *essential* in order for us to be the supernatural Church that God intends.**

CHAPTER TWO

EVIDENCES OF THE GRACE OF GOD

*P*aul's letter to the Corinthians reveals that the church in Corinth was *exploding* with an abundance of spiritual gifts. By studying First Corinthians 14, we discover that they were experiencing such an overflowing life of the Holy Spirit in their congregation that Paul felt compelled to write and instruct them on how to regulate such an abundance of spiritual manifestations. God's grace had been liberally poured out on these amazing converts to the Christian faith.

When the grace of God touches a person's life or the life of an entire church, it always produces transformation and has manifold effects. It can give a person the ability to repent, the desire to change, and the power to live an obedient and sanctified life. But as Paul began writing First Corinthians, he started out by specifically reminding the Corinthian believers of how the grace of God manifested among them *in spiritual gifts*. Yes, God's grace manifests in many ways in a believer's life, but Paul especially noted spiritual

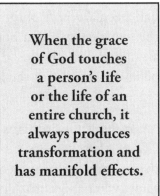

When the grace of God touches a person's life or the life of an entire church, it always produces transformation and has manifold effects.

gifts as *an outward evidence* that an amazing level of grace had been poured out on this particular congregation.

> **I thank my God always on your behalf, for the grace of God which is given you by Jesus Christ; that in every thing ye are enriched by him, in all utterance, and in all knowledge; even as the testimony of Christ was confirmed in you: so that ye come behind in no gift; waiting for the coming of our Lord Jesus Christ: who shall also confirm you unto the end, that ye may be blameless in the day of our Lord Jesus Christ. God is faithful, by whom ye were called unto the fellowship of his Son Jesus Christ our Lord.**
>
> **— 1 Corinthians 1:4-9**

In First Corinthians 1:4, Paul wrote, "I thank my God always on your behalf, for the grace of God which is given you by Christ Jesus."

In this verse and in the verses that follow, the apostle Paul began addressing the gifts of the Holy Spirit and explained why their operation is *essential* in the Church until the coming of Jesus. But before we venture further into the subject of spiritual gifts, it is first imperative that we look at this word "grace" to see what it meant to New Testament readers.

Paul began this subject by talking about how the grace of God had been *liberally poured out* on the church in Corinth — and the apostle explained how that grace had become visibly evident among them. In this discussion, we're going to see that Paul believed the gifts of the Holy Spirit were *outward evidences* of the grace of God.

In First Corinthians 1:4, Paul recalled that when people in Corinth first came to Christ, the grace of God was poured out on them. In order to understand Paul's statement, it's important to know what the word "grace" meant to a New Testament reader.

As already noted, there are manifold graces expressed through the life of a person who has been redeemed. However, if we stay with what Paul was saying in these particular verses, we can conclude that, in context, he was specifically referring to the gifts of the Holy Spirit. As we proceed in this book, we'll see that in this passage, Paul was specifically describing how grace *always* comes with some *outward evidence* or *visible manifestation* — and just as in the case of the Corinthians, these visible manifestations include an abundance of the gifts of the Holy Spirit.

In the Greek language of the New Testament, the word "grace" is *charis*. Pages and pages could be written about the origins and the various nuances of meaning contained in this one word. But one of these historical meanings of *charis* is significant for this discussion. This word *charis* sometimes denoted *special power that was conferred upon an individual or group of individuals by the gods*. Once this *charis* was conferred upon a person or group of people, it imparted to them *superhuman abilities*.[1] In other words, it enabled them to do what they could not normally or naturally do. In some secular literature from the early New Testament period, the word *charis* was even used to denote individuals who had been placed under a "magic spell" that transformed their personalities and imparted supernatural abilities to them.

As used in secular Greek literature, *charis* described a specific moment when an individual experienced a supernatural touch of the gods, always resulting in some type of *outward evidence* or *visible manifestation*. In this context, a person or group of people would never experience a supernatural impartation of *charis* without demonstrating *outward evidence*. Experiencing one without the other simply wasn't within the realm of possibility.

In the New Testament, the word "grace" — this same Greek word *charis* — is occasionally translated *favor* because a person

---

[1] James Orr, ed., *The International Standard Bible Encyclopedia,* "Grace," Vol. 2 (Grand Rapids, MI: Eerdmans Publishing Co., 1939), p. 548.

who receives *charis* has been *supernaturally enabled* as a result of receiving a manifestation of *favor* from God. So when we read of "grace" in the apostle Paul's writings, we can know that he was referring to God graciously imparting a special touch that *enables*, *empowers*, and *strengthens* the recipients. All of this aptly depicts the word "grace" and its effects on those who receive it. *It is a divine touch that transforms an individual and gives him the ability to do what he could not do before.*

All these facets of meaning are helpful to understand the word *charis* in the writings of the New Testament. We come to understand that when "grace" touches a person or a group of people, that divine impartation:

- *Enables*, *empowers*, and *strengthens* them.

- Enhances their personalities and imparts to them supernatural abilities.

- Is always accompanied by some type of *outward evidence or demonstration*. Grace is *never* silent or invisible.

> Grace first produces *inward change*, but it also always comes with *outward evidence*. It is never silent; it is never invisible; it always manifests in a visible way.

Of course, grace first produces *inward change*, but it also always comes with *outward evidence*. It is never silent; it is never invisible; it always manifests in a visible way. In the case of the Corinthian believers, when God's grace touched them, it became visible through the many supernatural manifestations and gifts of the Holy Spirit that operated in their midst.

Likewise, if you have been touched by God's grace — and as a believer, you *have been* touched by this grace — you should expect His grace to visibly show up in many areas of your life as an outcome. Grace will empower you to have victory over sin. It will enable you to control your tongue. And it will transform you as its influence changes your behavior.

By studying Paul's epistle to the Corinthian church, we find a specific insight regarding this truth. When God's grace has been liberally poured out, it often visibly shows up in the form of the gifts of the Holy Spirit as they begin to operate in a believer's life. Once again, God's grace *always* comes with an outward, visible demonstration. And in First Corinthians 1:4-9, the apostle Paul clearly taught that one byproduct of this divine impartation of grace is the overflowing operation of the gifts of the Holy Spirit in the life of a believer or congregation.

I urge you to think back to the time you first came to Christ and to consider how your life began to change from that moment forward. You know now that God's grace always comes with outward proof and visible manifestations — and that His grace is an empowering touch that enables you to be and do what you could have never been or done before. So ask yourself:

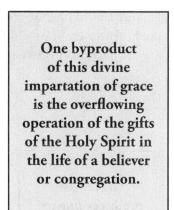

One byproduct of this divine impartation of grace is the overflowing operation of the gifts of the Holy Spirit in the life of a believer or congregation.

- *How did this divine grace show up in my life when I first repented and came to Christ?*

- *What changed in my life that revealed the reality of God's grace that had been poured out on me?*

- *How has this grace been visibly demonstrated in my walk with God since I was born again?*

As we continue to discover more of what the Holy Spirit was saying through Paul in First Corinthians 1:4-9, keep in mind these crucial points about God's grace:

- It produces outward evidence.

- It enables you to be what you previously could never be.

- It empowers you to do what you naturally could never do.

- It causes a normal, natural human being to be able to operate in the supernatural.

One of the ways the Holy Spirit visibly manifested in the church of Corinth was by a rich display of spiritual gifts. We're going to explore First Corinthians 1:4-9 further to see that this is also one of the primary ways the grace of God appears when it has touched any child of God or congregation of believers.

CHAPTER THREE

BECOMING
SPIRITUALLY WEALTHY

*H*ow would you like to have so many spiritual gifts operating in your church that your church family was considered to be spiritually wealthy? That's exactly what Paul said was a reality in the church at Corinth. As Paul continued writing to the church at Corinth, he expounded further about how the grace of God demonstrated itself among the Corinthian believers: "That in every thing ye are *enriched* by him…" (1 Corinthians 1:5).

The word "enriched" in this verse is a translation of the Greek word *plousios*, a word that describes *vast wealth*. That word *plousios* is where we get that word "plutocrat," which refers to *a person who is so rich that he is unable to ascertain the full extent of his own wealth* or *a person whose power is derived from his wealth*. This person's investments and companies, as well as the percentage of interest he earns on his portfolio, all grow so rapidly that his accountants and bookkeepers find it impossible to keep track of how much wealth he actually possesses. In addition, the vast wealth the plutocrat possesses positions him to exercise power in his realm of influence.

Paul used this word *plousios* in First Corinthians 1:5 to tell the church at Corinth — and us — that we are "enriched" by the Lord. The Greek word for "by" in this verse is *en*, which in this verse can mean either *in him* or *by him*. This conveys two very powerful truths to you and me about the enriching power of the grace of God:

1. The day we were born again and placed *into Jesus Christ* was the richest day of our lives. On that day, we literally became *joint heirs* with Jesus Christ, with a legal right to all the promises of God! Indeed, that was an infinitely rich day for each of us! In light of this, First Corinthians 1:5 could be interpreted, *"We were made rich the day we were placed into Him...."*

2. But the Greek word *en* could also emphasize the point that this enrichment process isn't a one-time event; it continues throughout our lives as we walk with God. The verse could thus be interpreted, *"We are continually being enriched as a result of being in Him...."*

3. Because the word *plousios* is used, this verse conveys the following idea: *"You are invested with great spiritual riches because you are in Him — and that's not all! The longer you remain in Him, you just keep getting blessed with more and more wealth that comes from being in Him."*

Of course, Paul was talking about *spiritual* riches, not *worldly* riches. As time progressed, the word *plousios* came to depict riches in a more general sense, including the riches of honor, wisdom, mercy, and so on.

First Corinthians 1:5 uses the word *plousios* to happily proclaim that the Corinthian church was "enriched" with gifts of the Spirit, such as:

- The gifts of utterance — *tongues, interpretation of tongues,* and *prophecy*

- The gifts of revelation — *the word of knowledge, the word of wisdom, and discerning of spirits*

As you will see in Chapter Four, there are three other gifts of the Spirit in addition to these, but these that I've just shared were the categories of spiritual gifts that especially flourished in the Corinthian church.

The church of Corinth was *loaded* with these kinds of spiritual gifts. In fact, these gifts were in such mighty manifestation in Corinth that Paul had to write the church about how to *manage* such a huge abundance of spiritual gifts in their assemblies (*see* 1 Corinthians chapters 12-14). As you will soon see, the Corinthian believers had more of these gifts in manifestation than any other church of that time. In a real sense, they were *extremely wealthy* in regard to these special spiritual manifestations.

The Corinthians had been enriched when they first came to Christ, becoming joint-heirs with Jesus Christ and inheritors of the promises of God. But by remaining in Jesus, they were constantly made richer in demonstrations of God's manifested power as the gifts of the Spirit operated mightily among them.

By using this word "enriched," Paul categorically stated that the Corinthian believers were so lavishly endowed with spiritual riches that it was impossible to calculate the extent of it. They had become familiar with the power of the Holy Spirit's manifested presence through these spiritual gifts that had been deposited in them by the grace of God. Based on the meaning of this Greek word *plousios*, you could say they were *spiritual plutocrats*.

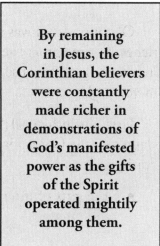

By remaining in Jesus, the Corinthian believers were constantly made richer in demonstrations of God's manifested power as the gifts of the Spirit operated mightily among them.

Paul noted that the Corinthian believers were especially enriched because of the vast number of spiritual gifts that operated among them. These spiritual gifts were *outward evidences* and *visible manifestations* proving that the grace of God had been liberally poured out on them and that the power of God was operating in their midst.

The Bible teaches that God is no respecter of persons. What His grace did among the Corinthians is exactly what it will do for every person and congregation that has an open heart to yield to the working of His Spirit in their midst. When His grace comes upon an ordinary person or congregation, it literally spills over into all types of outward manifestations of the Holy Spirit's power, which includes spiritual gifts.

> **What God's grace did among the Corinthians is exactly what it will do for every person and congregation that has an open heart to yield to the working of His Spirit in their midst.**

The gifts of the Spirit bring spiritual riches into our lives. In fact, the more these gifts operate, the richer and more powerful we become spiritually!

That explains why there were so many spiritual gifts in the church at Corinth. God's grace had been mightily poured out among them, and that outpouring of divine grace resulted in spiritual gifts of every kind.

But just what *are* the gifts of the Holy Spirit? We'll discuss the answer to that question in the next chapter.

CHAPTER FOUR

WHAT EXACTLY ARE
THE GIFTS OF THE SPIRIT?

*I*n First Corinthians 12, Paul unequivocally stated that the gifts of the Holy Spirit are *manifestations of the Holy Spirit* to the Church. He wrote in verse 7, "But the manifestation of the Spirit is given to every man to profit withal," and then proceeded to list those gifts or manifestations.

If these gifts are manifestations of the *Holy Spirit*, they must be good, because the Holy Spirit does only what is good and profitable for us. In addition, this verse plainly tells us the Holy Spirit doesn't want to just be present in the Church; He wants to *manifest* Himself in the Church — and one way He manifests Himself is through spiritual gifts.

Paul further stated that the nine gifts of the Spirit are designed by God to operate in "every man." The words "every man" is from the Greek word *hekastos,* which is an all-inclusive term that includes *every single person with no one excluded.* It plainly means that God wants *every* Christian to function in spiritual gifts. And "no one

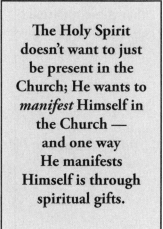

The Holy Spirit doesn't want to just be present in the Church; He wants to *manifest* Himself in the Church — and one way He manifests Himself is through spiritual gifts.

excluded" really does mean that *not one believer* is to miss out on receiving and operating in this vital part of his or her spiritual inheritance.

Yes, that means the Holy Spirit wants to manifest these gifts through *you*!

Paul continued to say that when these gifts are at work, they cause everyone to "profit." The Greek word for "profit" describes something that is a *benefit* or *an advantage gained*. This means the operation of spiritual gifts brings a true *benefit* to the Church and gives believers a supernatural advantage in their daily walk. The type of benefit these gifts provide is clearly described in First Corinthians 1:6, which we will study in the next chapter.

The devil knows that these spiritual gifts are beneficial and that they are instrumental in giving believers the advantage over him. That's the reason Satan has withstood their operation in the Church and even tried to theologically convince people that the gifts of the Spirit passed away with the death of the apostles. You see, the enemy knows that when a supernatural element of the Holy Spirit is at work in the Church, it brings a dimension of Christ to the Church that believers otherwise do not know. These manifestations of the Spirit are *essential* if the supernatural power of Christ is going to be demonstrated inside His Church.

> The devil knows that these spiritual gifts are beneficial and that they are instrumental in giving believers the advantage over him. That's the reason Satan has withstood their operation in the Church.

During the time Paul was writing to the Corinthian believers, there was a sundry of various spiritual gifts in operation in their midst. But in First Corinthians 1:5, Paul affirmed which gifts were most common in the church at Corinth. He says, "That in every thing ye are enriched by Him, in all *utterance*, and in all *knowledge*."

The word "utterance" is the Greek word *logos*, which in this context refers to *words that are vocalized*. The word "knowledge" is the Greek word *gnosis*, which is the Greek word for *knowledge* or *insight*. As used here, it referred to the *revelatory gifts* of the Holy Spirit that impart *supernatural knowledge* or *supernatural insight*.

In First Corinthians 12, Paul listed a broad range of spiritual gifts. Among these, he listed these *vocal gifts* and *revelatory gifts*. The vocal gifts include *tongues*, *the interpretation of tongues*, and *prophecy*. These are spiritual gifts that, when vocalized, supernaturally convey a message from the heart of God to a specific person or congregation. The church at Corinth was overflowing with these gifts of the Holy Spirit.

The revelatory gifts of the Holy Spirit include the *word of wisdom*, *word of knowledge*, and *discerning of spirits*. These are spiritual gifts that cause a person to supernaturally receive understanding from Heaven of something that could not be naturally obtained — or knowledge that is received *independently* of that which could be revealed naturally. These revelatory gifts were also demonstrated in abundance in the church at Corinth.

Paul's list of spiritual gifts in First Corinthians 12 includes three additional gifts of the Holy Spirit: the gifts of *faith*, *healings*, and *miracles*. However, we can conclude from Paul's words in First Corinthians chapter 14 that the gifts primarily operating among the Corinthian congregation were the *vocal gifts* and *revelatory gifts*.

Before we go on to discuss the nature of these nine gifts of the Spirit found in First Corinthians 12, it's good to note that there are variations of all these manifestations of the Holy's Spirit power. As Paul wrote in verses 4-7:

Now there are diversities of gifts, but the same Spirit. And there are differences of administrations, but the same Lord. And there are diversities of operations, but it is the same God which worketh all in all. But the manifestation of the Spirit is given to every man to profit withal.

The manifestations and operations of the Holy Spirit are endless in their variety and diversity, but the end result is always toward one end: *"to profit withal."* These nine gifts are always for our benefit. And because they originate from the Spirit of God, we can be assured that they are good and perfect gifts, because they come "from above" (*see* James 1:17).

THE NINE GIFTS OF THE HOLY SPIRIT

What you are about to read is not intended to be a thorough study of the gifts of the Spirit, but simply a starting point — with a brief definition for each gift and a scriptural example to illustrate how each gift operates. For a broader study of this subject, I recommend you read *The Holy Spirit and His Gifts Study Course* by Kenneth E. Hagin.

Let's take a look at each of these gifts one by one.

Word of Wisdom

In First Corinthians 12:8, Paul listed a spiritual gift that he called the "word of wisdom." The Greek word translated "word" in this context really refers to a *fragment* of wisdom. The word "wisdom" refers to *special insight* that is not naturally obtained.

Thus, the "word of wisdom" actually describes a gift that operates in that moment when *a fragment of special insight* is supernaturally revealed to an individual about a specific situation. It is received as "wisdom" because it delivers *an answer* or *a directive* to a pressing need, question, or situation, or it provides insight into future events that could not be known naturally.

Example: In Acts 27, the apostle Paul was on a ship with others that was headed directly for disaster. After the crew's long, futile struggle to bring the ship under control, Paul had a dream during the night in which he was told, "Fear not, Paul; thou must be brought before Caesar: and, lo, God hath given thee all them that sail with thee" (Acts 27:24). This information did not give Paul a full answer regarding his situation, but it was a "word" from Heaven that gave him direction and insight into the future for his situation. He supernaturally knew, at least in part, that all would be well, because he was destined to stand before Caesar in Rome. This is a wonderful example of a supernatural, fragmentary word of wisdom that both gave an answer to a believer for the pressing need of the moment and provided insight into an aspect of God's future plan and purpose for that believer.

> It was a "word" from Heaven that gave Paul direction and insight into the future for his situation. He supernaturally knew, at least in part, that all would be well, because he was destined to stand before Caesar in Rome.

Word of Knowledge

In First Corinthians 12:8, Paul also listed a spiritual gift that he calls the "word of knowledge." As we just saw, the Greek word translated "word" really refers to a *fragment* of knowledge in this context. Just as we saw that a word of wisdom describes wisdom not naturally obtained, the "word of knowledge" likewise refers to *a fragment of special knowledge* that one supernaturally receives.

This, then, is the ability to supernaturally know facts and details that would not be known in the natural. When a "word of knowledge" is given to a believer by the Holy Spirit, it is often imparted to illuminate listeners to God's intimate, personal involvement in the facts and details of a specific situation or in a person's life so that His purpose can be fulfilled in that situation or in that individual's life.

Example: When Jesus was at the well in Samaria, a woman came to draw water. When she spoke to Jesus, certain facts and details of her life were instantly revealed to Him as He spoke with her. Jesus didn't see every fact and detail about her life at that moment. But the fragments of personal information about this Samaritan woman that the Holy Spirit imparted to Jesus were precisely correct. And when He shared those supernaturally revealed details with her, the woman was immediately made aware of God's tender care for her (*see* John 4:5-30).

Special Faith or the Gift of Faith

In First Corinthians 12:9, Paul included "faith" in his list of spiritual gifts. This is not natural faith, which every person possesses. (In Romans 12:3, Paul clearly taught that *every person* is given a measure of faith.) In this context, Paul was referring to *special* faith, otherwise known as the *gift of faith*.

This spiritual gift is manifested as a sudden impartation by the Holy Spirit of supernatural, special faith at a critical moment to accomplish God's purpose or desire in a particular situation or event. When this supernatural burst of faith is suddenly released in a believer by the Spirit, that person is empowered to believe the impossible is doable in order to accomplish what can only be done supernaturally.

Example: In Acts 14, Paul was preaching to a group of pagans when he sensed a sudden release of special faith. In that moment, Paul called upon a lame man to stand and to walk. In obedience to Paul's command of special faith, the lame man arose and walked — completely made whole in an instant. Paul recognized the divine moment when the gift of special faith was in operation, and he acted on it. As a result, the impossible was manifested as a reality in the natural realm.

Gifts of Healing

In First Corinthians 12:9, Paul also listed "gifts of healing" as a gift of the Spirit. It is significant that the word "gifts" is plural, because it tells us that there are different aspects of this spiritual manifestation — all of them designed to produce healing, but in sundry ways.

> Paul recognized the divine moment when the gift of special faith was in operation, and he acted on it. As a result, the impossible was manifested as a reality in the natural realm.

It is also noteworthy that the word "healing" is the Greek word *iaomai*, which means *to cure*. This word would even describe being *doctored* by a physician. This is important, because a medical doctor doesn't normally produce instantaneous results for his patient; rather, he prescribes medicine or orders some procedure that eventually cures the one needing to be healed. Likewise, this gift of the Holy Spirit is very often a supernatural cure that begins with a prayer and at times the laying on of hands, but the healing may take full effect over a period of time. Although divine in nature, the word "healing" used here nonetheless refers to a progressive result.

Example: In Luke 17, a group of lepers met Jesus as He entered a certain village to seek His healing touch. As you will see in the following example, the "working of miracles" occurs when the laws of nature are overridden, and what could never occur in the natural *suddenly* and *instantly* takes place. A miracle is not what happened with that group of lepers. Luke 17:14 clearly says these lepers were healed and cleansed "as they went." This was a manifestation of a gift of healing — a supernatural touch of the Holy Spirit that generally occurs over a period of time and that ultimately cures a person from his ailment.

Working of Miracles

In First Corinthians 12:10, Paul went on to list the "working of miracles" as a gift that the Holy Spirit distributes as He wills. The Greek text actually says "the operation of powers." With this phrase, Paul described a divine operation of supernatural power that overrides natural laws and quickly does what is naturally impossible.

When pertaining to the human body, the "working of miracles" usually occurs in a split second — when, for example, a damaged organ or limb is instantly and supernaturally healed or restored. God's power suddenly speeds up a healing process that would normally take place over a long period of time or that would perhaps never naturally occur — and in a blink of an eye, the process is miraculously complete.

> In a split second, the atoms in the water solidified for Jesus to walk on a firm path. This was the power of God overriding natural laws.

Another example of the working of miracles would be a supernatural overriding of the laws of nature that enables one to do what no human could naturally do. An example of this occurred when Jesus walked on the water. In a split second, the atoms in that water solidified for Jesus to walk on a firm path. This was the power of God overriding natural laws.

Example: Another instance when "working of miracles" occurred was the multiplication of the loaves and fishes. This spiritual gift operated through Jesus at a critical moment when the power of God instantly transformed and supernaturally multiplied the small portions of food Jesus held in His hands. Although the instantaneous multiplication of physical matter is impossible in the natural realm, the power of God overrode the laws of nature and enabled the impossible to miraculously come to pass.

Prophecy

In First Corinthians 12:10, Paul next listed "prophecy" as a gift of the Spirit that God intends to operate in the Church until the Jesus' return for His Church. The word "prophecy" is a Greek word that means *to speak on behalf of God*; *to speak in advance of a situation*; *to foretell an event*; or *to assert the mind of God to others*.

It is important to note that one who speaks a prophetic word to the church is not necessarily called into the full-time ministry of a prophet. In First Corinthians 14:1, Paul encouraged *everyone* to seek this spiritual gift, and in verse 31, he stated that *everyone* can prophesy. Over and over in Scripture, we can see that this simple gift of prophecy manifested to comfort those under duress, bring encouragement to people's hearts, and redirect their attention to God.

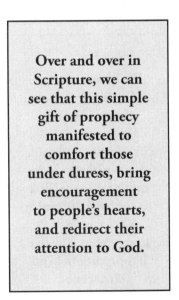

Over and over in Scripture, we can see that this simple gift of prophecy manifested to comfort those under duress, bring encouragement to people's hearts, and redirect their attention to God.

According to First Corinthians 14:3, the primary objective of this spiritual gift is to impart *edification, exhortation*, and *comfort* to the listeners. When a person moves in this spiritual gift, he or she is divinely inspired to speak on behalf of God and to deliver a message He wants to convey to His people at a particular time or for a particular situation. The operation of this spiritual gift results in an individual or congregation receiving new understanding about a truth, insight, or directive from the heart of God that helps strengthen, encourage, and instruct the listeners so they can walk with Him more accurately.

Example: An example of the gift of prophecy is found in the event that occurred when the elders of Antioch gathered for a time of fasting and prayer. Acts 13:2 says, "As they ministered to the Lord, and fasted, the Holy Ghost said, Separate me Barnabas and Saul for the work whereunto I have called them." According to this verse, the gift of prophecy was at work as the Holy Spirit spoke through someone in the group. And when the Spirit spoke, that word from the Lord launched Paul and Barnabas out into their apostolic ministries.

Discerning of Spirits

Paul also listed "discerning of spirits" as a gift of the Spirit in First Corinthians 12:10. The Greek words for "discerning of spirits" actually describe one's supernatural ability to perceive the true nature of a spiritual situation or to discern what spiritual forces are really at work in the life of an individual or in a specific circumstance.

> The manifestation of this gift occurs in an instant. It is as though a curtain has suddenly been pulled apart and one is enabled to see into the realm of the spirit to know what is really happening behind the scenes.

This revelatory gift is a supernatural revealing or discerning of spiritual forces that otherwise cannot be naturally discerned. The manifestation of this gift occurs in an instant. It is as though a curtain has suddenly been pulled apart and one is enabled to see into the realm of the spirit to know what is really happening behind the scenes or to see or perceive the genuine spiritual condition that is otherwise hidden to the eyes.

This gift often manifests in spiritual leaders, since leaders need this grace-given equipment to supernaturally perceive what kind of spiritual influence people are yielding to. The discerning of spirits is a vital piece of spiritual equipment given to leaders as the Holy Spirit wills to aid in the selection of a leadership team, in leading others through difficult situations, and in accurately seeing the true nature of a particular spiritual environment.

Example: In Matthew 9, Jesus was speaking with a group of scribes, and it seemed that they were listening with open hearts. But suddenly Jesus supernaturally knew what He otherwise would not naturally know. He literally "saw" or discerned what was occurring inside these scribes spiritually, and He confronted them. Matthew 9:4 says, "And Jesus knowing their thoughts said, Wherefore think ye evil in your hearts?" Although the people tried to conceal their true thoughts, the gift of discerning of spirits enabled Jesus to supernaturally perceive or see the actual spiritual forces He was dealing with.

Divers Kinds of Tongues

In First Corinthians 12:10, Paul stated that "divers kinds of tongues" is another gift that the Holy Spirit distributes as He wills for the edification of the Church. In this phrase, Paul described the public gift of tongues, which is different from a devotional tongue that one uses in prayer — often referred to in this modern day as a heavenly "prayer language." Also, praying in tongues "publicly," or as a corporate group, is not a manifestation of this gift of "divers kinds of tongues."

Paul was explicitly referring here to that moment when someone is moved supernaturally by the Holy Spirit's inner prompting to deliver a specific message in tongues from the heart of God to an individual or an assembled group.

According to First Corinthians 14:5, Paul taught that when a public message in tongues is interpreted, which we will discuss next, it brings supernatural edification to the Church. Some try to discount this particular gift as a less important gift of the Spirit, but Paul listed it alongside the other spiritual gifts, ranking it equal in importance to the others.

Example: The best scriptural reference to "divers kinds of tongues" is found in Paul's discussion of this gift in First Corinthians 14, where the apostle taught about how to properly flow in the manifestation of this spiritual gift and where he charged that no one forbid its operation. If you want to know more about "divers kinds of tongues," it is imperative that you do a serious and thoughtful study of First Corinthians 14.

Interpretation of Tongues

Finally, in First Corinthians 12:10, Paul mentioned "the interpretation of tongues" as a ninth gift of the Holy Spirit. This gift operates in cooperation with "divers kinds of tongues." When one is inspired to speak a public message in tongues, that vocal gift of the Spirit must be accompanied by a second vocal gift, the gift of interpretation (*see* 1 Corinthians 14:26-28).

It must be pointed out that this particular gift is not the *translation* of tongues; it is the *interpretation* of tongues. One who moves in this spiritual gift supernaturally understands and speaks out the meaning of the message in tongues that has been spoken. The person may not understand what was said in tongues word for word, but he has the supernaturally imparted ability to interpret it — in other words, to give public voice to what God desires to communicate. The length of the interpretation may not necessarily match the length of the message in tongues, because this is a Spirit-inspired interpretation rather than a word-for-word translation.

This gift of interpretation of tongues, then, necessarily works in partnership with divers kinds of tongues. Again, this is not a reference to a corporate group publicly praying in tongues together; it refers to the moment when an individual is inspired by the Spirit to deliver a distinct, public message in tongues. Such a message requires public interpretation, and for that to occur, the gift of interpretation must be present and active.

Example: Once again, for a deeper understanding of the interpretation of tongues, it is best to refer to Paul's instructions in First Corinthians 14, which covers the operation of this gift in-depth. The church at Corinth had the gift of "divers kinds of tongues" in regular manifestation. Therefore, Paul wrote to help guide and instruct the Corinthian congregation on how to properly flow in the gift of interpretation as a necessary accompaniment to the gift of "divers kinds of tongues."

I want to add that the gifts of the Spirit often work in pairs or in groupings. For example, where the working of miracles is at work, it is often accompanied by special faith — and these two gifts working together can move mountains of opposition that literally are *impossible* to move in the natural realm. When the word of knowledge is in operation, it is often accompanied by the gifts of healing and the working of miracles. The breadth and variety of how these spiritual-gift combinations can manifest is manifold, but it is helpful to realize that

> **Where the working of miracles is at work, it is often accompanied by special faith — and these two gifts working together can move mountains of opposition that literally are *impossible* to move in the natural realm.**

wherever one of these spiritual gifts operates, it often does so in partnership with one of the other gifts.

The church at Corinth was so "enriched" with these spiritual manifestations that Paul felt it necessary to write an *entire "chapter"* in his first letter to this congregation about how to manage the operation of these spiritual gifts (*see* 1 Corinthians 14). *Imagine that* — so many of these gifts were in operation in a single Corinthian church service that the church had to be instructed on how to properly manage them!

Today we're thankful if we see just *one* of these gifts in operation in a church service! But we are hungry to see more!

IS IT RIGHT OR WRONG TO SEEK SPIRITUAL GIFTS?

Many who were reared in traditional churches have been taught that it is wrong to *seek* spiritual gifts. But if these spiritual gifts are from God, why would it be wrong to seek them? If they really are God-given manifestations of the Holy Spirit, shouldn't we earnestly desire for them to work among us?

It must be noted that Paul never rebuked or corrected the Corinthian believers for having so many spiritual gifts or for seeking God for their manifestation. In fact, in First Corinthians 14:1, Paul instructed them to "desire" spiritual gifts. In that verse Paul says, "Follow after love and *desire* spiritual gifts...."

The first part of the verse contains a command: that we are supposed to ardently follow after love. No one would argue that we are to pursue having loving relationships with others. But if we believe the first part of the verse, we must take the *entire* verse as ours to obey. That means we must also embrace the part that *commands* us to "desire" spiritual gifts.

The Greek word for "desire" means *to be fervently boiling with zealousness* for the object desired. It depicts *an intense desire that causes one to seek something until it is obtained.* This is not a mere want or wish. This Greek word emphatically means that Paul wanted the church of Corinth to have an *intense longing* and a *boiling zealousness* to experience more and more of these spiritual manifestations in their midst. Paul knew spiritual gifts were vital to bring the supernatural dimension of Christ to that church, and that is why he *really* wanted the Corinthian Christians to *fervently boil with desire* and *to seek* for them.

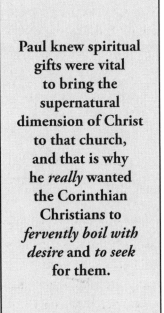

Paul knew spiritual gifts were vital to bring the supernatural dimension of Christ to that church, and that is why he *really* wanted the Corinthian Christians to *fervently boil with desire* and *to seek* for them.

Since God's Word is true throughout all generations, we can know that the Holy Spirit through the apostle Paul was also telling us in First Corinthians 14:1 to desire spiritual gifts. God is encouraging us to follow after love and to fervently desire the operation of spiritual gifts in our lives and in our churches.

But why *are* the gifts of the Spirit so important that He would tell us to zealously desire them? We'll see the answer to this question in the next chapter.

CHAPTER FIVE

A SUPERNATURAL DIMENSION OF CHRIST IN THE CHURCH

*A*s Paul continued writing about the gifts of the Holy Spirit in the church at Corinth, he stated that as a result of the operation of these gifts, "the testimony of Christ was confirmed" among them (1 Corinthians 1:6).

I want to begin explaining the meaning of this verse with a story from Russia, where I have lived with my family for decades.

The State Hermitage is the most famous of all Russian museums. It is located on the banks of the Neva River in St. Petersburg, Russia. Within its walls is a huge collection of religious paintings that were collected mostly from the time of Catherine the Great. This museum, the former Winter Palace of the Russian czars, is fabulous beyond description and attracts millions of visitors who come to view this world-renowned art collection and to see the opulence in which the czars lived.

The first time I visited the Hermitage was near the end of the time of the Soviet Union; thus, Communism and atheism were still dominant forces in the nations that comprised the former USSR. As I walked past the section of paintings by Rembrandt, I saw the painting of Lazarus being raised from the dead by Jesus. The painting was so moving that it drew me nearer to observe the painting up close. Then I read the plaque on the base of the frame, which said, "The Fairy Tale of Jesus Christ Raising Lazarus From the Dead." I was stunned that Lazarus' resurrection was referred to as a fairy tale.

But as I moved from that painting of Jesus to others that depicted scenes from His life, I realized that they were all officially identified as various "fairy tales of Jesus Christ." By calling the works of Jesus "fairy tales," it was an attempt to put the Gospel on the same level as Peter Pan, Little Red Riding Hood, etc.

My experience in the museum that day caused me to start thinking in another direction. I began to consider how so much about Jesus Christ really is a fairy tale to many people — including Christians who grew up in church and who faithfully read their Bible and love the Lord today. When they read about the miracles He performed, they relegate His miracle-working power to a limited time frame that is long past and to a people who are no longer alive. They then conclude that they cannot expect such miracles today. Consequently, the only thing believers in this category really know regarding Jesus' power is what they have read in the Bible.

Never having personally witnessed Jesus' miracle-working power, these Christians can only fantasize and try to imagine what His miracles must have been like. As a result, much of what they know about Jesus is purely mental, imaginary, or speculative — similar to the way they might view the hero in a fairy tale or legend.

But God never intended for Jesus to be only a historical figure who did something in the past. Jesus is alive *today*, and through the ministry of the Holy Spirit and His gifts, Jesus brings His supernatural reality right into the midst of the local church! This is why Paul told the Corinthians, "...In everything ye are enriched by him, in all utterance, and in all knowledge; even as the testimony of Christ was confirmed in you" (1 Corinthians 1:5,6).

As we have seen in previous chapters, the Corinthian church was endowed with so many spiritual gifts that Paul says they were "enriched" with them. They were particularly enriched with gifts of utterance and knowledge. As mentioned earlier, the word "utterance" refers to the vocal gifts, such as tongues, interpretation of tongues, and prophecy. Knowledge gifts refers to the revelatory gifts, such as the word of wisdom, the word of knowledge, and the discerning of spirits. Prophecy could also fall into this category when it includes a revelatory gift in its message.

Paul said that these gifts "confirmed" the "testimony" of Christ among the Corinthian believers (*see* 1 Corinthians 1:6). The word "confirmed" is the Greek word *bebaioo*, which means *to make firm, concrete, or stable*; *to authenticate*; *to verify*; *to guarantee*; or *to prove to be true*.

The word "testimony" is from the Greek word *maturios*, and it describes *a personal testimony that is so strong, it could stand up to scrutiny in a court of law.* But when a "testimony" (*maturios*) is "confirmed" (*bebaioo*), it is extra powerful! Now we not only have a witness — that is, a person or a group of people who possess concrete knowledge and facts — but we also have confirming evidence brought forth to validate their knowledge and verify that their report is bona fide truth.

> **God never intended for Jesus to be only a historical figure who did something in the past. Jesus is alive *today*, and through the ministry of the Holy Spirit and His gifts, Jesus brings His supernatural reality right into the midst of the local church!**

Now let's connect this concept to the gifts of the Spirit in the Corinthian church. According to Paul's account, the believers in that church were *enriched, loaded, and mightily endowed* with the gifts of the Spirit. These gifts, he said, *confirmed the testimony* of Jesus Christ in their midst.

What did the Corinthian believers know of Jesus Christ? What was the testimony they possessed and proclaimed about Him? From a historical perspective, they had been taught and therefore knew that:

- Jesus was a Prophet.

- Jesus was a Healer.

- Jesus was a Miracle-Worker.

However, the Corinthian congregation didn't just intellectually know these things about Jesus because of books they had read. They *experientially knew Him* in these roles because the gifts of the Spirit literally *activated* and *authenticated* what they had learned about Jesus.

- By means of the Holy Spirit's manifestations, Jesus the Prophet operated before the Corinthian believers in their church services. They didn't need to fantasize about what Jesus the Prophet was like, because He regularly operated in their midst in that role through the gift of prophecy.

- The Corinthian believers didn't have to try to imagine what it had been like when Jesus healed the sick, because the gifts of healing functioned among them, causing them to experientially know Jesus the Healer.

- There was no reason for the church in Corinth to speculate about what it must have been like to see Jesus' miracles, for these believers had the working of miracles operating in their church services, making Jesus the Miracle-Worker a reality to them.

The gifts of the Spirit lifted Jesus right off the pages of history and brought Him into the midst of the Corinthian church services. That is what the gifts of the Spirit are designed to do for us in *this* day as well. They remove Jesus from a purely historical, fairy-tale category and bring Him right before our eyes so we come to know Him and His power experientially!

First Corinthians 1:6
could thus be taken to mean:

"Everything you've heard and believed about Jesus Christ has been authenticated, proven beyond a shadow of a doubt, verified, and guaranteed to be true because of the gifts of the Spirit."

This means that if there is no operation of the Holy Spirit's gifts in your life or in the church you attend, the demonstration of an entire supernatural dimension of Jesus Christ is missing from your life and church. Your mind may be filled with accurate information, and that is always a good thing. But God never intended for your salvation to exist only on an intellectual level. He gave the Holy Spirit to the Church to bring the overflowing, abundant life of Jesus Christ right into the midst of His people!

The bottom line is this: *There is a whole new level of understanding regarding Jesus — who He is and how He operates — that can only be comprehended by experiencing and participating in the gifts of the Holy Spirit.*

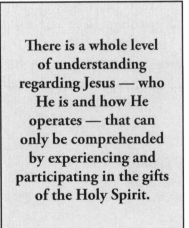

There is a whole level of understanding regarding Jesus — who He is and how He operates — that can only be comprehended by experiencing and participating in the gifts of the Holy Spirit.

First Corinthians 1:6 emphatically means that the Holy Spirit wants to confirm everything you intellectually know about Jesus. The Spirit of God wants you to know Jesus the Prophet, Jesus the Healer, and Jesus the Miracle-Worker. When the gifts of the Holy Spirit operate through you or on your behalf through someone else, they give testimony to the fact that Jesus is still alive, still healing, and still working miracles today. Thus, by means of these marvelous spiritual gifts, the Holy Spirit authenticates Jesus Christ to you on a greater and a deeper level.

So are you ready for the Jesus of the Bible to step off the pages of history, right into your life and into the life of your church? If your answer is yes, ask the Holy Spirit to start moving supernaturally in your midst through the gifts of the Spirit. Earnestly desire spiritual gifts to operate, and steadfastly set your faith for their manifestation as the Holy Spirit wills.

> **If you sense an inner nudge to step out in faith and allow the Holy Spirit to use you in these spiritual gifts, don't hesitate to obey.** *He is speaking to you.*

And if you sense an inner nudge to step out in faith and allow the Holy Spirit to use you in these spiritual gifts, don't hesitate to obey. *He is speaking to you.* The Spirit of God wants you to step forth and allow Him to work supernaturally through *you*!

CHAPTER SIX

HOW MANY GIFTS OF THE HOLY SPIRIT ARE TOO MANY?

*T*he gifts of the Spirit were so abundant in the church at Corinth that, according to the apostle Paul in First Corinthians 1:7, the believers in that church were *second to none* in regard to these spiritual manifestations. In First Corinthians 1:7, Paul wrote, "So that ye come behind in no gift...." In other words, Paul was stating that they were *first* among all the churches when it came to the vast number of spiritual gifts and supernatural manifestations that operated among them.

The phrase "come behind" includes a translation of the Greek word *husteros*, which by itself describes *a lack* or *a falling short* of something and represents a *deficiency in* or *a coming behind of* a person or a group of people. When applied, it would mean this person or group of people is *inferior* in comparison to others or even *depleted* of whatever is needed and therefore *insufficient* to meet needs that are presented to them.

If Paul had used this word *husteros* by itself, it would have meant the church at Corinth was *inferior* to other churches in respect to the gifts of the Spirit. However, that is emphatically *not* what Paul said in First Corinthians 1:7. Instead, he emphatically stated that they were not *husteros* in regard to spiritual gifts. This means that not only were the Corinthian believers *not* inferior, but they were in fact *superior* when it came to the gifts of the Holy Spirit. They were fully operational, fully supplied, and thoroughly furnished when it came to spiritual gifts and manifestations. These believers were so abundantly blessed in regard to the gifts of the Holy Spirit that Paul affirmed they were *second to none* in this respect.

Based on Paul's words in First Corinthians 1:7, we know that the church in Corinth had more supernatural spiritual manifestations in operation than any other church in the First Century. If a special conference had been held to teach on the gifts of the Holy Spirit, it probably would have been conducted in Corinth because no church had more gifts or understanding about how to operate in the gifts of the Spirit than the Corinthian church. They were simply the *premier example* to all other churches when it came to this subject.

In First Corinthians 1:7, Paul concretely stated that the Corinthian believers lacked no "gift." The word "gift" is a translation of the Greek word *charisma*. It is derived from *charis*, the Greek word for *grace*, which we covered in Chapter Two. When *charis* becomes *charisma*, it depicts *something that is given or imparted by grace*. This is why certain people call themselves *Charismatics*. The name indicates that they believe the gifts of the Holy Spirit have been *imparted* to them, or at least that they place a significant emphasis on the gifts of the Spirit in their expression of worship.

Historically, the word *charisma* was used to describe that moment when the gods *graced* or *donated* supernatural *ability*, *favor*, or *power* to an individual. Thus, this word *charisma* meant a *gracious gift* — and that is exactly how it should be interpreted in the New Testament. A person who has had a *charisma* imparted to him or her has received a *donation* or an *enablement* from God that equips that person in some supernatural manner.

This tells us that because these magnificent gifts of the Holy Spirit are grace-given, there is no room for boasting or self-glory in our possession of them, for they are not natural talents developed by our own ability. These are supernatural graces that are divinely imparted by the Spirit of God.

Paul's words in First Corinthians 1:7 tell us that every known gift of the Spirit was in manifestation in the Corinthian congregation. This local body of believers was simply overflowing with these demonstrations of the Spirit. We can see this in the way Paul described their times of assembling together: "How is it then, brethren? when ye come together, every one of you hath a psalm, hath a doctrine, hath a tongue, hath a revelation, hath an interpretation. Let all things be done unto edifying" (1 Corinthians 14:26).

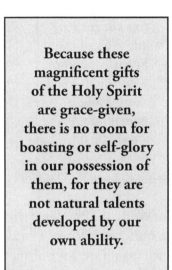

> Because these magnificent gifts of the Holy Spirit are grace-given, there is no room for boasting or self-glory in our possession of them, for they are not natural talents developed by our own ability.

Paul's wording is significant in First Corinthians 14:26. He stated that "every one" of the believers in that church had a gift, implying that everyone came to the meeting ready to operate in spiritual gifts. As noted in the previous chapter, Paul never corrected or rebuked the believers of Corinth for this abundance. In fact, the wording of this verse suggests that he was thankful for the divine operation of spiritual gifts that existed among them.

Paul also said, "...Let all things be done unto edifying." Notice the first part of this phrase: "...Let *all* things be done...." Paul's words clearly meant that *all* of these things *should be done* and *were necessary* in the Church. As far as Paul was concerned, the gifts of the Spirit were not optional — operating in spiritual gifts *should* be done. In fact, the apostle wrote the entire chapter of First Corinthians 14 to teach the Corinthian believers how to accommodate the various gifts of the Spirit, urging them not to forbid the Holy Spirit's operations.

> As far as Paul was concerned, the gifts of the Spirit were not optional — operating in spiritual gifts *should* be done.

In verse 12, Paul described the zealousness of these believers for spiritual gifts. He said, "Even so ye, forasmuch as ye are zealous of spiritual gifts, seek that ye may excel to the edifying of the church." Paul *affirmed* the zealous desire of the Corinthian congregation. But in addition, he told them that the purpose of these spiritual manifestations must always be for the "edifying" of the Church.

The word "edifying" is an architectural or construction word that refers to the *enlarging* and *improving* of a building. When a person decides, for example, to construct a new room on his house, thus enlarging and improving his house, he first settles on a design before he proceeds. A lot of thought goes into the home-improvement project. Once the plan is determined, it is carefully followed as the addition to the house is built little by little and the designer's dreams are realized.

By using this word "edification" in First Corinthians 14:12 — from a Greek word that means *enlarging* and *improving* a building or structure — Paul emphasized two very important principles:

- We must mentally decide that we are going to make room for the Holy Spirit to move among us. If we haven't made this decision before, we must determine what God desires for us regarding spiritual gifts; then we must begin to follow our convictions and permit these supernatural manifestations to function.

- As we allow the Holy Spirit to work in this supernatural way among us, He will use the divine working of His gifts to spiritually enlarge us and improve our ability to walk in the power of the Spirit as He walked on the earth.

Used in this context in First Corinthians 14:12, the word "edification" tells us something important. When the gifts of the Holy Spirit are allowed to freely operate in a fitting and proper way, these divinely given manifestations *improve* the Church spiritually. Instead of making people immature, as some have wrongly suggested, Paul clearly stated that the gifts of the Holy Spirit bring growth and spiritual enlargement to the Church.

Paul's primary guiding principle for the operation of these spiritual gifts is found in First Corinthians 14:40. In that often quoted verse, Paul taught that whenever and wherever the gifts of the Spirit are in manifestation, all must be done "decently and in order." Here we have the most important rule regarding what is acceptable and appropriate in the operation of the Holy Spirit's gifts.

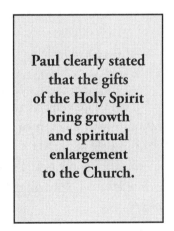

Paul clearly stated that the gifts of the Holy Spirit bring growth and spiritual enlargement to the Church.

What does "decently and in order" mean? The word "decently" is the Greek word *euschemonos*. Other than this verse, the word *euschemonos* is only found two other times in the New Testament — in Romans 13:13 and in First Thessalonians 4:12. In both of these places, it is translated *to do something honestly* or *to walk honestly*. It carries the notion of something that is done *properly* as opposed to *improperly*. It has to do with *intent* and *motivation* more than outward action.

The word "order" is the Greek word *taksis*. It carries the idea of *something done in a fitting way* or *something done according to order*. The Jewish historian Josephus used the word *taksis* when he recorded the way in which the Roman army erected their camps — indicating their camps were *orderly* and *well-planned*. The commanders didn't engage in last-minute planning. Their camps were not hastily thrown together; rather, they were set up in an *organized* and *thoughtful* manner.

Josephus also uses the word *taksis* to describe the way the Essene Jews were respectful of others. These Jews would wait until others were finished speaking before they'd take their turn and speak out. In Josephus' depiction of this behavior among the Essenes, he used the word *taksis* to picture people who were *respectful, deferential, courteous, accommodating, well-mannered,* and *polite.*

Taking these meanings into account, First Corinthians 14:40 could be translated:

"Let everything be done in a fitting and proper manner — one that is organized, well-planned, respectful, and polite."

This verse tells us that even the gifts of the Holy Spirit should be manifested in an orderly, respectful, and polite manner. Paul's simple rule was that one shouldn't interrupt or raise his voice to speak above others. Rather, each person should wait until the other is done speaking before he ventures to give what is on his heart.

Paul gave further instruction along this line in First Corinthians 14:29-33: "Let the prophets speak two or three, and let the other judge. If *any thing* be revealed to another that sitteth by, let the first hold his peace. For ye may all prophesy one by one, that all may learn, and all may be comforted. And the spirits of the prophets are subject to the prophets. For God is not the author of confusion, but of peace, as in all churches of the saints."

In these verses, Paul recognized and affirmed that a multiplicity of manifestations may occur in a single meeting. He simply asked that those who spoke by the Spirit would refrain from interrupting others before they were finished.

Thus, Paul was making clear that we can control how the gifts of the Spirit manifest through us. Even as we begin to yield to the Holy Spirit's prompting to be used in spiritual gifts, it is not necessary to be impolite. This is an example of what Paul meant when he wrote that we are to do things decently and in order.

HOW MANY GIFTS ARE TOO MANY?

Someone may ask, "When it comes to spiritual gifts operating in a local church, how many are too many?" Since they are the gifts *of the Holy Spirit*, this would be like asking, "How much of the Holy Spirit is too much?" The answer, of course, is that we want *all* that the Holy Spirit has to give us!

In the church at Corinth, where the gifts of the Holy Spirit were being demonstrated in abundant measure among the people, Paul never even inferred that there were too many spiritual gifts in operation. Instead, he actually encouraged the Corinthian believers to *desire* spiritual gifts (*see* 1 Corinthians 14:1). In addition, Paul simply asked that everything be done in a fitting and proper manner that is organized, well-planned, well-mannered, and polite.

Most congregations today do not need to worry that they have too many spiritual gifts in operation. Most are asking for *more* of these gifts to be manifested, *not* less. Hungry hearts are crying out

61

for a greater demonstration of the supernatural presence of Jesus Christ in the Church.

We shouldn't waste time fearing that too many gifts of the Spirit will start operating in our midst as we pursue more of Jesus. That is usually *not* the case in most modern churches today. Instead, we should focus on learning how to more effectively allow the Holy Spirit to work in our midst! Then, like the church at Corinth, we will begin to be enriched with an abundance of spiritual gifts in actual manifestation. And as we do, we will manage the operation of the gifts of the Spirit in our midst in a fitting and orderly way, as the Scripture commands us to do.

> Hungry hearts are crying out for a greater demonstration of the supernatural presence of Jesus Christ in the Church.

It is impossible to have too much of anything that comes from the Holy Spirit. Whatever He has to give is good, beneficial, and transforming. Let's open our hearts and cry out in faith for a greater demonstration of His powerful gifts among us. Oh, that it could also be said that *we* were *second to none* regarding the operation of these powerful gifts!

CHAPTER SEVEN

THE POWER TO STRENGTHEN AND ESTABLISH

*A*s Paul continued to elaborate on the gifts of the Holy Spirit, he stressed the truth that God intends for these gifts to function in the Church until the return of Christ. We find this truth in First Corinthians 1:7, where Paul wrote, "So that ye come behind in no gift; waiting for the coming of the Lord Jesus Christ."

In this verse, Paul confirmed that the gifts of the Holy Spirit will be active and functional in the Body of Christ until the end of the Church Age when Jesus returns. This means the claim that these gifts and manifestations ceased with the death of the apostles is entirely *untrue*.

Those educated in Church history would never argue about whether or not these supernatural manifestations have been in operation throughout more than 2,000 years of the Church's existence. There are abundant historical records to affirm that these gifts have *never* ceased. The attempt to rationalize away the gifts of the Holy Spirit by saying they ceased with the death of the apostles is therefore intellectually dishonest and historically inaccurate.

But in addition to what history shows, First Corinthians 1:7 clearly states that *all* the gifts of the Spirit will be in manifestation and operate in the Church until the revelation of Jesus Christ at His next coming. We see, then, that the New Testament emphatically teaches that there will *never* be a cessation of the gifts of the Holy Spirit. Paul avowed that they will be fully operational until the end of the Church Age — a moment on God's timeline that is still *before* us.

> The New Testament emphatically teaches that there will *never* be a cessation of the gifts of the Holy Spirit. Paul avowed that they will be fully operational until the end of the Church Age — a moment on God's timeline that is still *before* us.

In First Corinthians 1:8, Paul went on to tell us the benefit that these supernatural gifts bring to each of us and to the larger Body of Christ. Rather than make us weak and silly, as some suggest, Paul stated that the gifts of the Holy Spirit are necessary to *strengthen* and *establish* us. He wrote, "Who shall also confirm you unto the end, that ye may be blameless in the day of our Lord Jesus Christ."

There are three very important words in this verse regarding the impact of the gifts of the Holy Spirit in the life of an individual or a congregation. The words "confirm," "end," and "blameless" are vital to understanding the long-term effect of spiritual gifts. Let's see what these words meant when Paul wrote this verse and how they should be applied in our lives now as they pertain to the gifts of the Holy Spirit.

As we saw in Chapter Five, the word "confirm" is a translation of the Greek word *bebaioo*, which means *sure, fixed, steadfast*, or *maintaining firmness*. In classical Greek, the word *bebaioo* meant *firm, durable, unshakeable, sure, reliable,* or *certain.* In the legal sense, this word was used to depict a document that was *valid, certain, proven, and guaranteed.* In its broadest sense, *bebaioo* meant *fit, certain,* or *reliable,* and pictured *someone standing firm on his feet.*

The use of this word *bebaioo,* as it is used in verse 8 in connection with the gifts of the Holy Spirit, tells us that these gifts make us *firm, durable, unshakeable, sure, reliable, certain,* and *fit.* So rather than make us spiritually silly or weak, as some suggest, spiritual gifts actually help us *stand firm on our feet!*

The word "end" in verse 8 is a translation of the Greek word *telos,* a Greek word that in this verse describes something that is *mature* or *fully ripened.* Thus, Paul was not describing the "end" of something in this verse — such as the end of an era — as the *King James Version* seems to insinuate. Instead, the apostle used the Greek word *telos* to describe the working of steadfast growth and endurance in believers' lives — by these demonstrations of the gifts of the Spirit — to the end that these believers become *"ripened"* or *fully mature.*

The use of the word *telos* in this verse — as it pertains to the gifts of the Holy Spirit — reveals God's purpose for these gifts: They are intended to help bring us to a higher realm of spiritual maturity. If these supernatural gifts are operating according to God's design, they cultivate a state of *ripeness* in the believer's walk with the Lord and a greater *maturity* of the Church at large. Paul's words mean that there is actually an entire dimension of spiritual

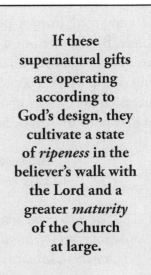

If these supernatural gifts are operating according to God's design, they cultivate a state of *ripeness* in the believer's walk with the Lord and a greater *maturity* of the Church at large.

maturity that cannot be achieved without the operation of spiritual gifts. We can conclude, then, that the gifts of the Spirit are *essential* for the Body of Christ to attain "…unto the measure of the stature of the fulness of Christ" (Ephesians 4:13).

The third word we'll look at in First Corinthians 1:8 — "blameless" — is a translation of the word *anegkletos*, an old Greek word that means *having no blot on one's life for which one could be accused, arraigned, or disqualified*. It is legal language that describes *one who has been found spotless or unimpeachable*. Not even a hint of accusation can be found against this individual. Thus, he is "blameless."

So in the use of the word *anegkletos* in this verse in connection with the gifts of the Holy Spirit, we discover another facet of God's divine design for these gifts: They are meant to bring us to a place of *conviction, holiness,* and *personal integrity*.

When spiritual gifts are working in the life of a believer or a congregation, they often expose deficiencies and produce repentance. As a result, character is purged and justifiable accusation is expunged from a person's life or from the midst of a local body. By the operation of these spiritual gifts, people are often so impacted that their character and reputation become transformed and impeccable. People's lives that may have previously been susceptible to accusation and blame have changed course and are on a new path toward becoming unimpeachable.

The combined use of these words in this verse could be taken to mean:

"These gifts make you fit, firm, and unshakeable. They put you on your feet spiritually and lead you into new levels of spiritual maturity. Ultimately, these gifts will work to produce unimpeachable character in you...."

As we read this expanded translation of First Corinthians 1:8, it becomes clear why we need the gifts of the Holy Spirit working among us. And we see in this verse why the apostle Paul said they *must* be in manifestation until the return of Jesus Christ. If these supernatural gifts are that vital, then God would of course never allow them to cease! They are essential for us to reach the spiritual maturity that He has designed for His Church.

When these divine enablements are released in our midst and allowed to operate as the Holy Spirit intends, they literally bring a *supernatural partnership* with Jesus Christ into the Church that we as believers otherwise would never know. God has provided the avenue by which we can experience this divine partnership in these last days, but we have a vital part to play. It's up to us to learn to lean on the Holy Spirit — and this *must* include embracing the gifts of the Holy Spirit as He works among us. This wonderful privilege God has afforded us to partner with the Head of the Church is the subject of the next chapter!

> When these divine enablements are released in our midst and allowed to operate as the Holy Spirit intends, they literally bring a *supernatural partnership* with Jesus Christ into the Church that we as believers otherwise would never know.

CHAPTER EIGHT

A SUPERNATURAL PARTNERSHIP WITH JESUS CHRIST

*A*s Paul continued to write about the gifts of the Holy Spirit in First Corinthians 1, he made a significant point that I mentioned in the last chapter. Paul stated that where these gifts are in operation, a believer or a local church will experience a supernatural *partnership* with Jesus Christ on a level that can only be experienced *if* the gifts of the Holy Spirit are in operation.

However, before we proceed further to see what Paul said about this supernatural partnership, let's first review the main truths we've discussed up to this point to make sure we understand them in their proper context. Let's take First Corinthians 1:4-9 verse by verse, and review what Paul was saying to us:

> **"I thank my God always on your behalf, for the grace of God which is given you by Jesus Christ..." (v. 4).**

In this verse, Paul described the marvelous, empowering grace that was poured out on the church at Corinth. We saw in Chapter Two that the word "grace" — the Greek word *charis* — always denotes an empowering touch that comes with some type of outward manifestation. In the case of the Corinthians, God's graceful touch came, in part, with a manifestation of spiritual gifts.

"That in every thing ye are enriched by him, in all utterance, and in all knowledge…" (v. 5).

Here in verse 5, Paul affirmed that the grace of God enriched the Corinthian congregation with spiritual gifts and spiritual manifestations. According to this verse, they were particularly rich with gifts of utterance and knowledge. These included *vocal gifts*, such as *prophecy, tongues*, and *interpretation of tongues* — and *revelatory gifts*, such as *word of wisdom, word of knowledge*, and *discerning of spirits*. These were not all the gifts of the Spirit in operation in Corinth, as Paul stated in verse 7 that *all* the gifts of the Spirit were in operation among them. However, there was especially an abundance of *these* types in that church.

"Even as the testimony of Christ was confirmed in you…" (v. 6).

Paul taught in verse 6 that the gifts of the Holy Spirit are necessary to bring the testimony of who Jesus is right into our midst. We may mentally know a lot about Christ, but much of this knowledge remains in the mental realm *until* the gifts of the Holy Spirit work among us.

> We may mentally know a lot about Christ, but much of this knowledge remains in the mental realm *until* the gifts of the Holy Spirit work among us.

When the gifts of healing, for example, are in operation, these manifestations give believers practical experience with Christ the Healer. As a result, Christ is no longer just a historical Healer from the past, but also a present-day Healer. In this way, the gifts of healing "confirm the testimony" of Christ the Healer among the saints.

In this way, each gift of the Holy Spirit gives God's people practical experience with a facet of Jesus Christ in a way that supersedes mental knowledge.

"So that ye come behind in no gift; waiting for the coming of our Lord Jesus Christ..." (v. 7).

According to this verse, it is not possible to have too many gifts of the Holy Spirit in operation in a local church. There may need to be rules as to how to *administer* them, but to have too many gifts of the Spirit in operation is simply impossible. In the verse just stated, Paul clearly expressed that the church at Corinth had no shortage of gifts.

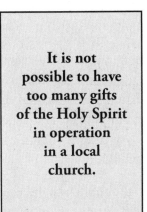

It is not possible to have too many gifts of the Holy Spirit in operation in a local church.

Paul furthermore announced that God intends for these divine manifestations to be fully functioning in the Church until the next coming of Jesus Christ.

"Who shall also confirm you unto the end, that ye may be blameless in the day of our Lord Jesus Christ..." (v. 8).

In this verse, Paul stated that the gifts of the Holy Spirit are necessary to strengthen and establish us and to bring believers and local churches into new levels of spiritual maturity. Paul additionally affirmed that whenever these gifts operate as God intended, they assist to expunge sin and remove spiritual deficiencies from a believer or congregation. So rather than make a believer or congregation silly or immature, these gifts are actually essential in bringing a believer or a local church into spiritual *maturity*.

"God is faithful, by whom ye were called unto the fellowship of his Son Jesus Christ our Lord" (v. 9).

Paul concluded this powerful section of Scripture about the gifts of the Holy Spirit by affirming in verse 9 that the operation of these divine gifts brings every believer and every church into a unique "fellowship" with Jesus Christ. What does the word "fellowship" mean in this context where Paul is discussing spiritual gifts?

Let's look at the word "fellowship" to see what it is in Greek. The word "fellowship" is from the Greek word *koinonia* — a word that has several flavors of meanings.

One primary meaning of the word *koinonia* is that of *partnership*. A premier example of this meaning can be found in Luke 5:6 following the miraculous catch of fish that Jesus supplied. After the fishermen had fished all night and caught nothing, Jesus told them to cast their nets on the other side. When they obeyed, they caught such a massive number of fish that the nets began to break!

Peter knew he couldn't handle this miraculous catch by himself, so he called to other fishermen in nearby boats to come and assist him. Luke 5:7 says, "And they beckoned unto their *partners*, which were in the other ship, that they should come and help them. And they came, and filled both the ships, so that they began to sink."

> Paul stated that the gifts of the Holy Spirit are necessary to strengthen and establish us and to bring believers and local churches into new levels of spiritual maturity.

The word "partners" in this verse is a form of this word *koinonia*. However, in Luke 5:7, it refers to *real business partners*. These were not theoretical partners; *they were true, legitimate business partners.* The form of the Greek word *koinonia* used in this context lets us know that Peter was no small-time fisherman. He owned an entire fishing enterprise, and those men in the other boats were his *business associates* or his *company partners*. Whether these other fishermen were co-owners or employees who worked for Peter, the men were all working together on the same job and were focused on a joint venture to catch and sell fish. They were in *partnership* with Peter.

Now take this understanding into your study of First Corinthians 1:9. In this verse, Paul used this word *koinonia* to describe how Jesus *partners* with any church where the gifts of the Holy Spirit are in operation. Of course, Jesus is present and partnering with every congregation, but Paul in this verse implied that the gifts of the Holy Spirit bring a believer or a local church into a special level of *partnership* with Christ.

Paul wrote, "…By whom ye were called unto the fellowship of his Son Jesus Christ our Lord" (v. 9). That word "fellowship" actually carries the idea of *"partnership"* — emphatically declaring that when the gifts of the Holy Spirit are operating in the Church, they cause Jesus to supernaturally partner with the Church in a greater dimension.

For example, a pastor can preach dynamically on the subject of healing, but when the gifts of healing suddenly manifest at the end of his message and people are supernaturally healed, this gift sets people free and demonstrates the truth of the message.

Mark 16:20 says it like this: "And they [the early preachers] went forth, and preached every where, the Lord working with them, and confirming the word with signs following."

In this verse, we see the Lord partnering with the early believers by confirming the Word they preached through signs following — which means the nine gifts of the Spirit were in operation. What if there had been no "signs following"? The message would have been true nonetheless; however, the supernatural confirmation gave strength to the message that was preached. In this way, Christ *partnered* with the early ministers of the Gospel through the ministry of the Holy Spirit.

Hebrews 2:4 is another scripture along this line. It states, "God also bearing them witness, both with signs and wonders, and with divers miracles, and gifts of the Holy Ghost...." Again, we see Jesus partnering with those who proclaim the Gospel message. Without supernatural confirmation, the message would have been true — but God knew that supernatural confirmation was needed for the sake of the hearers. When these gifts of the Holy Spirit operated in conjunction with the preaching of the Gospel, they provided a tangible demonstration of this supernatural *partnership* of Jesus Christ with the Early Church.

> **Just as the early believers partnered with Jesus on this supernatural level, we also must learn to partner with Him by yielding to and cooperating with the ministry of the Holy Spirit.**

Just as the early believers partnered with Jesus on this supernatural level, we also must learn to partner with Him by yielding to and cooperating with the ministry of the Holy Spirit. The power of God and the gifts of the Holy Spirit are the same as they were 2,000 years ago — and if we will learn to work with the Spirit and to know His ways, these mighty manifestations will become more and more evident among God's people today. Rather than dream about what it was like 2,000 years ago, let's open our hearts to the Holy Spirit today and allow Him to work among us as He did so mightily in the early years of the Church!

CHAPTER NINE

GOD WANTS TO USE *YOU* IN SPIRITUAL GIFTS!

*I*n First Peter 4:10, Peter wrote, "As *every man* hath received the gift...." In this verse, Peter is referring to the spiritual enablements each believer has received from the Lord that empowers him or her to minister to others.

The phrase "every man" is translated from the Greek word *hekastos*, which we looked at briefly in Chapter Four. It is an all-inclusive word that literally means *every single person, no one excluded*. This undeniably means that every person who has been born of the Spirit and who declares that Jesus is Lord has been supernaturally graced or endowed from on High with divine gifts — including the gifts of the Spirit we have been studying in this book.

Because the word *hekastos* is used, it emphatically means that *no one is excluded* from these God-given gifts. Even the person with the lowest self-esteem is mightily gifted by the Spirit of God; he is simply unaware of the powerful gifts that reside within him.

If you think that *you're* not gifted, you are wrong! The usage of the word *hekastos* in First Peter 4:10 clearly means that you, too, are endowed with magnificent, God-given gifts.

The apostle Peter went on to say, "As every man hath *received* the gift...." The word "received" in this verse comes from the Greek word *lambano*, which means *to receive into one's possession* or *to take into one's own control and ownership*. It carries the idea of *taking hold of something, grasping onto something,* or *embracing something so tightly that it becomes your very own.* As Peter used it in this verse, it means that God sees it as our responsibility *to accept and take ownership of these gifts as our own.*

Then Peter wrote, "As every man hath received *the gift....*" As noted above, the word "gift" in this verse is the word *charisma,* derived from the word *charis,* the Greek word for *grace,* which we studied in Chapter Two. However, when the word *charis* becomes *charisma,* it doesn't describe only grace, but it speaks of *grace-given gifts.* Specifically, the word *charisma* was used in secular literature during New Testament times to denote individuals who were graced and favored by the gods with a divine touch that enabled them supernaturally. The *charisma* they received didn't just internally make them better; it equipped them with supernatural abilities that were manifested externally.

Peter correctly used this word to describe how "every man," or every believer, has been divinely touched by God once he or she is placed into Christ. As a result, Peter declared, every believer has been supernaturally favored with supernatural giftings. This could refer to an entire range of enablements — which includes our topic of discussion, the gifts of the Holy Spirit.

From a linguistic point of view, the word *charisma* speaks of supernatural, God-given, grace-imparted, supernatural gifts, given by the Holy Spirit to "every man" that is in Christ. If you have been born again, this, of course, includes *you!*

Peter continued, "As every man hath received the gift, even so *minister* the same one to another...." The word "minister" comes from the Greek word *diakoneo.* This word portrays *a servant whose primary responsibility is to serve food and wait on tables.* It presents a picture of a waiter who painstakingly attends to the needs and wishes of the patron. It is this servant's supreme task to please clients; therefore, he serves honorably, pleasurably, and in a fashion that makes the people he waits on feel as if they are nobility. *This is a committed, professional server who is zealously dedicated to doing his job on the highest level possible.*

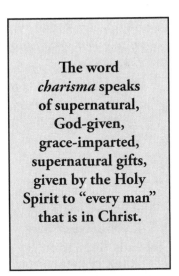

The word *charisma* speaks of supernatural, God-given, grace-imparted, supernatural gifts, given by the Holy Spirit to "every man" that is in Christ.

By choosing this Greek word *diakoneo*, Peter alerted us that God expects us to be passionately committed to using the gifts He has given us in such a way that pleases Him and meets the needs of others. That is why Peter continued by saying, "As every man hath received the gift, so let him minister the same *one to another....*" God intends for us to use these divine gifts to minister to one another. These gifts are never given for self-glory or self-promotion, but for the benefit of the larger Christian community and the world around us.

Peter concluded verse 10 by saying, "As every man hath received the gift, so let him minister the same one to another, as good *stewards* of the manifold grace of God." The word "steward" is from the Greek word *oikonomos* and was specifically used to describe the *household manager* for an upper-class, wealthy home. By using the word *oikonomos* in this verse, Peter informed us that God has made us the stewards of His own personal treasures. That means He expects us to give Him glory by allowing these gifts to operate through us to meet the needs of those around us.

Taking all of these Greek words into consideration, we could paraphrase this verse to read:

"Every single one of you without exception has received a grace-given gift. Embrace what God has placed inside you. Take ownership of it, and do your best to develop and use that gift to meet the needs of one another. God has entrusted a great deal to you by placing such a special gift in your life, and He is depending on you to be faithful with this important responsibility."

Make the decision if you haven't already done so to yield to the Holy Spirit's leading and to release the divine gifts God has placed inside you.

God gives you gifts and talents, and He expects you to let them operate through you for the purpose of meeting the needs of those around you. So make the decision if you haven't already done so to yield to the Holy Spirit's leading and to release the divine gifts God has placed inside you. Those gifts are inside your spirit, just waiting for you to step out in obedience when the Holy Spirit prompts you so they can begin to manifest for the blessing and benefit of others!

CHAPTER TEN

LET'S BE LOGICAL
ABOUT THIS!

*T*he following information is presented here as a way to make you think a little deeper about the importance of the gifts of the Holy Spirit in the Church. Stay with me as I walk you through a few initial thoughts that will lead you to a logical conclusion.

Just for a moment, let me deviate from the subject of spiritual gifts and talk about *water baptism* and *Communion*. You'll soon understand why I am doing this in the context of discussing the gifts of the Holy Spirit.

For approximately 2,000 years, the Church has practiced water baptism and Communion. But I suggest that you do a study comparing the number of verses about spiritual gifts in the New Testament with the number of verses about water baptism and Communion. If you do, I'll tell you what you will discover: There is only a small number of verses that actually address water baptism and Communion compared to the *vast* number of verses that address the subject of spiritual gifts.

For example, in the entire New Testament, there are only approximately *23* references or passages that address the subject of water baptism (*see* Matthew 3:13-16, 28:19; Mark 16:16; Luke 3:7,21, 7:29; John 4:1; Acts 2:38-41, 8:12,13,38,39, 9:18, 10:48,

16:15,33,19:5; Romans 6:3-5; 1 Corinthians 1:15-17, 15:29; Ephesians 4:5). Yet for 2,000 years, the Church has dogmatically and correctly taught that water baptism is a requirement for every serious disciple of Jesus Christ. No one would question the importance of water baptism, even with this relatively minimal number of verses that deal with the subject.

But what makes this even more interesting is that there is not a single verse in the entire New Testament telling us *how* to conduct this important act of faith and scriptural rite of the Church. Imagine something so important as water baptism — yet absolutely no instructions are given in the New Testament about how to do it!

Similarly, there are only *28 references* in the entire writings of the New Testament that address the subject of Communion (*see* Matthew 26:26-29; Mark 14:22-25; Luke 22:19,20; John 13:2; Acts 2:42; 1 Corinthians 10:16-21; 11:23-33). Yet we firmly believe in Communion and practice it regularly with heartfelt faith and commitment. No one who loves Jesus and His Church would deny the important role that Communion plays in the Body of Christ.

It seems logical to assume that since Communion has such a significant purpose in the life of the Church, there would be a substantial number of verses in the New Testament committed to this subject — but this is simply not the case. And just as it is amazing that the New Testament gives no instruction on how to perform water baptism, it is also a striking fact that absolutely no guidelines are given anywhere in the New Testament about how to administrate the Communion elements. It's difficult to imagine that something so central to our faith as the celebration of Communion would have absolutely no instruction about how to practically do it, but that is exactly the case!

Now let's go back to the subject of spiritual gifts in this context. If you count the verses in the New Testament epistles that address the subject of *the manifold, grace-given gifts of the Holy Spirit* (including the fivefold ministry gifts, the motivational gifts, and the nine gifts of the Spirit we are discussing in this book) and also give concrete, well-established guidelines on how these gifts should operate in the Church, you will discover there are *103 verses* that fit this description (*see, for example,* Romans 1:11; 12:5-8; 1 Corinthians 1:5-9; 12:1-31; 13:1-13; 14:1-40; Ephesians 4:11-13; 1 Timothy 1:18; 4:14; 2 Timothy 1:6; Hebrews 2:4; 1 Peter 4:10,11, etc.).

Throughout the epistles of the New Testament, but particularly in the writings of Paul and Peter, the Scriptures deal extensively with the subject of spiritual gifts. And unlike water baptism and Communion, the New Testament includes explicit teaching on the gifts of the Spirit, even providing practical guidelines on how the gifts of the Spirit should operate in the local church. In fact, as noted earlier, the entire chapter of First Corinthians 14 is devoted to practical instruction about the gifts of the Spirit. This is noteworthy, considering the fact that there's not a single verse in the New Testament that provides practical instruction on how to conduct water baptism or administer Communion (except for Paul's lone admonition in First Corinthians 11:27-34 on the *attitude* of believers in receiving the elements).

What conclusions can we draw from these comparisons?

First, statistically, it means that the writers of the New Testament wrote about the operation and administration of spiritual gifts *four* times more than the subject of water baptism and almost *four* times more than the subject of Communion.

Second, let's not forget that this matter of spiritual gifts was such a priority to the Holy Spirit working through the apostle Paul that the entire chapter of First Corinthians 14 was written to give practical advice and suggestions about how the nine gifts of the Spirit should operate in the local church. Consider this point in light of the fact that Paul never wrote about how to perform water baptism or administer Communion. It should speak volumes to us about the importance that Paul — and the Holy Spirit *through* Paul — placed on the gifts of the Holy Spirit and the prominent role these gifts should have in the life of every believer and every congregation.

> This matter of spiritual gifts was such a priority to the Holy Spirit working through the apostle Paul that the entire chapter of First Corinthians 14 was written to give practical advice and suggestions about how these gifts should operate in the local church.

Just for a moment, let's put away any doctrinal preconceptions and look at this from a purely statistical, logical point of view.

Isn't it true that we would never question whether or not we are to practice water baptism and Communion? We believe in these demonstrations of our faith and practice them with deep reverence. Yet people often "argue" that the gifts of the Spirit are unnecessary or optional. They do this even though the gifts of the Spirit are statistically more prominently discussed in the New Testament! If people would look objectively at the number of scriptures that address spiritual gifts as compared to scriptures addressing water baptism and Communion, they might very well reach the conclusion that the gifts of the Spirit should carry at *least* equal importance than these other two practices of the Church!

God is a good Steward of all things, including *space* in the New Testament! If the gifts of the Holy Spirit were going to "pass away" with the death of the apostles, as some teach, or if they were relatively less important than these other subjects mentioned, why would God commit so much space in the New Testament to this subject?

Is it logical to think that God would include so many verses on this subject of spiritual gifts in the writings of the New Testament if He knew these gifts were short-lived and would soon pass away, only to impact a few who lived in the First Century? Why would He include such a large reservoir of instruction on spiritual gifts if it would all just be meaningless information of mere historical value with no application to the Church of all generations — information that would shortly need to be explained away?

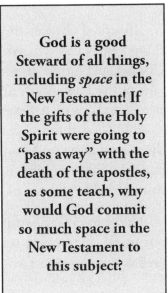

God is a good Steward of all things, including *space* in the New Testament! If the gifts of the Holy Spirit were going to "pass away" with the death of the apostles, as some teach, why would God commit so much space in the New Testament to this subject?

The argument that the gifts of the Spirit *passed away* or that they are *optional* is simply nonsense. God would not commit so much space in Scripture to a dead or even an optional issue. Remember, the New Testament teaches on the subject of spiritual gifts, or God-given graces, nearly *four times* more than water baptism and Communion. This alerts us to the fact that God expects the gifts of the Spirit to be manifested in abundance in the Church for the duration of the Church Age. As we saw in Chapter Seven, God expects these supernatural manifestations to be in operation until the return of Jesus Christ because they are *required* for the Church to be strong throughout all generations!

Is there any other logical way to explain why God would commit so much space to spiritual gifts in the New Testament — His personal "instructional manual" to us that He knew we would read and build our lives upon? Based on statistics alone, we should easily see that this is a very important subject in the mind of God.

CONCLUSION

This final chapter simply adds an exclamation mark to everything else we discussed earlier from Paul's first epistle to the Corinthian church. It is *imperative* that we take a fresh look at the gifts of the Holy Spirit and the important role they are to play in the life of every believer and in the experience of every local church! One thing is certain: God gave them because we need them to mature and empower us in our life in Christ — *not* to make us silly or childish, as that is *never* God's purpose in anything that He gives to us.

God's intention is for the reality of Jesus Christ to thrive in our midst. He doesn't want us to just know Christ intellectually. God longs for Jesus to step off the pages of the New Testament right into the midst of our lives and our church gatherings. In order for this to occur, we must open our hearts to the work of the Holy Spirit. It is the Holy Spirit and His gifts that will make this supernatural partnership of Jesus Christ a continual, day-by-day reality for us.

> God expects these gifts to be manifested in abundance in the Church for the duration of the Church Age.

As you finish the last pages of this book, I just want to remind you one more time of the title of this book: *Why We Need the Gifts of the Holy Spirit*. I pray that you now have a fresh and deeper understanding of why God gave these gifts to the Church and why they *must* operate among us until Christ's return.

I urge you — don't just add this teaching to the mental stack of information you already possess. Open your heart, and begin to act on what the apostle Paul urged every believer to do in First Corinthians 14:1. Actively desire and pray for an abundant manifestation of spiritual gifts operating in your life, in your local church, and in the larger Body of Christ. And let the motive of your heart continually be to reflect the heart of Jesus. Every gift and every demonstration of power is for the furtherance of His Kingdom and for the blessing and benefit of the people He died to redeem.

> **Don't just add this teaching to the mental stack of information you already possess. Open your heart and begin to act on what the apostle Paul urged every believer to do in First Corinthians 14:1.**

PRAYER TO RECEIVE
THE BAPTISM IN THE HOLY SPIRIT

The baptism in the Holy Spirit is a free gift to *everyone* who has made Jesus Savior and Lord of his or her life (*see* Acts 2:39).

After you made Jesus your Lord at the time of the new birth, the Holy Spirit came to live inside you, and your old, unregenerate spirit was made completely new. This subsequent gift is the "baptism into," or *an immersion in*, the Holy Spirit.

The baptism in the Holy Spirit supplies the supernatural power of God for witnessing about Christ, for enjoying a deeper, more intimate relationship with the Holy Spirit, and for victorious Christian living.

Receiving this precious gift is easy. Before you pray to receive the infilling of the Holy Spirit, you might want to read and meditate on the Scripture references I provide on the next page. Then expect to receive what you asked for *the moment* you pray!

If you would like to be baptized in the Holy Spirit and speak with new tongues (*see* Acts 2:4), simply pray the following prayer and then act on it!

Lord, You gave the Holy Spirit to Your Church to help us fulfill the Great Commission. I ask You in faith for this free gift, and I receive right now the baptism in the Holy Spirit. I believe that You hear me as I pray, and I thank You for baptizing me in the Holy Spirit with the evidence of speaking with a new, supernatural prayer language. Amen.

As a result of praying this prayer, *your life will never be the same.* You will have God's power working through you to witness, to operate in the gifts of the Holy Spirit, and to experience Jesus' victory as a living reality every day.

Rick Renner

Scripture References for Study and Review: Mark 16:17; Luke 24:39; Acts 1:4,5,8; 2:4,39; 10:45,46

REFERENCE BOOK LIST

1. *How To Use New Testament Greek Study Aids* by Walter Jerry Clark (Loizeaux Brothers).

2. *Strong's Exhaustive Concordance of the Bible* by James H. Strong.

3. *The Interlinear Greek-English New Testament* by George Ricker Berry (Baker Book House).

4. *The Englishman's Greek Concordance of the New Testament* by George Wigram (Hendrickson).

5. *New Thayer's Greek-English Lexicon of the New Testament* by Joseph Thayer (Hendrickson).

6. *The Expanded Vine's Expository Dictionary of New Testament Words* by W. E. Vine (Bethany).

7. *New International Dictionary of New Testament Theology* (*DNTT*); Colin Brown, editor (Zondervan).

8. *Theological Dictionary of the New Testament* (*TDNT*) by Geoffrey Bromiley; Gephard Kittle, editor (Eerdmans Publishing Co.).

9. *The New Analytical Greek Lexicon*; Wesley Perschbacher, editor (Hendrickson).

10. *The Linguistic Key to the Greek New Testament* by Fritz Rienecker and Cleon Rogers (Zondervan).

11. *Word Studies in the Greek New Testament* by Kenneth Wuest, 4 Volumes (Eerdmans).

12. *New Testament Words* by William Barclay (Westminster Press).

ABOUT THE AUTHOR

Rick Renner is a prolific author and a highly respected Bible teacher and leader in the international Christian community. Rick is the author of more than 30 books, including the bestsellers *Dressed To Kill* and *Sparkling Gems From the Greek, 1* and *2*, which have sold more than 3 million copies combined.

In 1991, Rick and his family moved to what is now the former Soviet Union. Today he is the senior pastor of the Moscow Good News Church and the founder of Media Mir, the first Christian television network in the former USSR that today broadcasts the Gospel to countless Russian-speaking and English-speaking viewers around the world via multiple satellites and the Internet. He is also the founder and president of Rick Renner Ministries, based in Tulsa, Oklahoma, and host to his TV program that is seen around the world. Rick leads this amazing work with his wife and lifelong ministry partner, Denise, along with the help of their sons and committed leadership team.

CONTACT RENNER MINISTRIES

For further information
about RENNER Ministries, please contact
the RENNER Ministries office nearest you,
or visit the ministry website at
www.renner.org.

**ALL USA
CORRESPONDENCE:**
RENNER Ministries
P. O. Box 702040
Tulsa, OK 74170-2040
(918) 496-3213
Or 1-800-RICK-593
Email: renner@renner.org
Website: www.renner.org

MOSCOW OFFICE:
RENNER Ministries
P. O. Box 789
Moscow 101000, Russia
+7 (495) 727-14-67
Email: partner@rickrenner.ru
Website: www.ignc.org

RIGA OFFICE:
RENNER Ministries
Unijas 99
Riga LV-1084, Latvia
+(371) 67802150
Email: info@goodnews.lv

KIEV OFFICE:
RENNER Ministries
P. O. Box 300
01001, Ukraine, Kiev
+38 (044) 451-8115
Email: partner@rickrenner.ru

OXFORD OFFICE:
RENNER Ministries
Box 7, 266 Banbury Road
Oxford OX2 7DL, England 44
+44 (0) 1865 355509
Email: europe@renner.org

THE HOLY SPIRIT AND YOU!

Working Together as Heaven's 'Dynamic Duo'

There is a *secret* place. A *partnership* of power. A place of *peace*. A wellspring of *living water* that enriches your life. This hidden fortress of power and peace is accessed when your spirit is in constant fellowship with the Holy Spirit. Together you are truly an unstoppable, dynamic duo.

The Holy Spirit dwells within you, and His purpose in your life includes equipping you with exactly *what* you need, *when* you need it. If He drops a thought into your mind to do something, do it. If He tells you something will work, it will work.

The Holy Spirit was the key to Jesus' ministerial success. And He is God's gift to you for *your* life journey!

$14.97 (paperback)
192 pages
ISBN: 978-1680311433

BOOKS BY RICK RENNER

Dream Thieves*
Dressed To Kill*
The Holy Spirit and You!* (formerly titled, *The Dynamic Duo*)
How To Receive Answers From Heaven*
Insights to Successful Leadership
Life in the Combat Zone*
A Light in Darkness, Volume One
The Love Test*
Merchandising the Anointing
No Room for Compromise, A Light in Darkness, Volume Two
Paid in Full*
The Point of No Return*
Repentance*
Say Yes!* (formerly titled, *If You Were God, Would You Choose You?*)
Seducing Spirits and Doctrines of Demons
Sparkling Gems From the Greek
    Daily Devotional 1*
Sparkling Gems From the Greek
    Daily Devotional 2*
Spiritual Weapons To Defeat the Enemy*
Ten Guidelines To Help You Achieve
    Your Long-Awaited Promotion!*
365 Days of Power*
Turn Your God-Given Dreams Into Reality*
Why We Need the Gifts of the Spirit*
You Can Get Over It*

*Digital version available for Kindle, Nook, iBook,
and other eBook formats.
Note: Books by Rick Renner are available for purchase at:
www.renner.org

The Harrison House Vision

Proclaiming the truth and the power
of the Gospel of Jesus Christ with excellence.
Challenging Christians
to live victoriously,
grow spiritually,
know God intimately.

Harrison House

Connect with us on

Facebook @ HarrisonHousePublishers

and Instagram @ HarrisonHousePublishing

so you can stay up to date with news

about our books and our authors.

Visit us at **www.harrisonhouse.com**

for a complete product listing as well as

monthly specials for wholesale distribution.